PBJO Publishing
Copyright © Pete Atkinson 2024

The right of Pete Atkinson to be identified as the Author of the Work has been asserted by him in accordance with the Copyright, Designs and Patent Act 1988.

All rights reserved. No part of this publication may be reproduced, stored in a retrieval system, or transmitted, in any form or by any means, electronic, mechanical, photocopying, recording or otherwise, without prior written permission.

Paperback ISBN 978-1-7385484-0-8
Hardback ISBN 978-1-7385484-1-5

Cover design copyright © Bethany Atkinson 2024

All italicised quotations are taken from the Holy Bible, New International Version Anglicised copyright © 1979, 1984, 2011 Biblica. Used by permission of Hodder & Stoughton Ltd, an Hachette UK company. All rights reserved. 'NIV' is a registered trademark of Biblica UK trademark number 1448790.

Scripture quotations marked (ESV) are from The ESV® Bible (The Holy Bible, English Standard Version®), copyright © 2001 by Crossway, a publishing ministry of Good News Publishers. Used by permission. All rights reserved.

Non-italicised words within italicised quotes indicate the author's own alteration, sometimes changing the tense or replacing an English word with a Hebrew or Greek equivalent.

EXPLORING ELOHIM'S EMBRACE

Who or What and Where is God?

Exploration Overview

INFINITE
Beyond Physicality
Pouring Out

"GOD IS..."
Love
Breath
Light

RELATIONSHIP
Community
Family
Lover

BLISS
Beauty
Peace
Life

LOGOS
Communication
Consciousness
Wisdom

WITH US
Collaboration
Emotion
Suffering

INFINITE
Paradoxical and Physical

It feels scary, dangerous –
not to mention impossible –
for the finite to attempt to describe the infinite.

But it also feels exhilarating, liberating –
not to mention necessary –
to explore…

Infinite

God is Infinite: Beyond Physicality

Since the beginning of civilisation, humans have tried to visualise the divine. Nearly every nation, kingdom, dynasty and empire has concocted their own pantheon of weird and wonderful looking gods. Superhuman or superanimal: all were represented visually, with many sculpted physically. Because humanity craves sight and touch.
In Christianity, God is described as a person – and humans are created in God's image. And when those two ideas are combined, it feeds the widespread image of God as some kind of ultra powerful human.
Someone like Santa.
Or a comic book superhero.
Or the bearded and muscular man painted on the Sistine chapel ceiling with his pointed, reaching finger. This renowned artwork bears a striking resemblance to Zeus, father of the Greek deities. Which is hardly surprising since much of early Christianity existed within a dominant Greek culture and the image of Zeus basically became muddled, mixed and merged with the God presented in the Bible.
The God revealed by Jesus was perceived through a Zeus-filter.
Viewed through a Zeus-lens.
Zeus was the Greeks' chief ruler of the skies. And the notion of God living high above us looking down – perhaps even firing down thunderbolts – remains common-place, heavily-baked, engrained within us.
Yet ever since humanity started exploring the far reaches of

our unfathomably enormous, expanding universe, the possibility of actually finding a supreme superbeing literally, physically dwelling above us was obliterated.

Disproved.

Rendered irrational.

Leading many to altogether dismiss belief in God.

But there is a better, healthier and truer way of conceptualising – and knowing – the chief father and ruler above and beyond us. Despite our human preference – perhaps reverence – for tangibility and visibility, the triune God of Christianity is both invisible and immaterial.

So when the Genesis creation narrative tells us that humanity was created in the image of God we can first think of humanity's intangible, immaterial attributes.

Our senses.

Our words.

Our energy.

Our thoughts.

Our emotions.

Our character.

The way we connect.

The way we give and share.

The way we are intimate.

The way we love.

The divine Elohim shares these non-solid human attributes. Or rather it's more accurate to say Elohim generously shares these divine attributes with us; they are an outpouring, spilling over from Elohim's embrace.

So when God is described as a person it's important that we don't subtly swap the word 'person' for 'human.' A clear distinction must be made: the communal Elohim is three persons – but not three humans. A human is a person with added physicality.

Indeed, it's easier to rationalise the Christian concept of the Trinity – the three in one and one in three – when we set ourselves free from trying to imagine three humans somehow becoming one, somehow squeezing into one body.

Abba, Yeshua and Ruach are three divine persons, not three divine superhumans. The three are one because they share the same divine attributes.

Divine characteristics.

The same divine nature, or essence.

'Yeshua' is the Hebrew name translated as Jesus. 'Ruach' is the Hebrew word for breath or air or spirit. And 'Abba' is the Aramaic word that Jesus agonisingly cried out in Gethsemane.[1] Together, united as one, they are 'Elohim,' the Hebrew word translated as 'God' in the opening chapter of Genesis. Mysteriously, 'Elohim' is a plural word, contrasting with the singular 'El.' And in the beginning, the creative Community of Elohim spoke using plural pronouns, agreeing with one heart and one mind: "*Let us make* humanity *in our image.*"[2]

This God who is more energetic-verb than static-noun crafted a visible and invisible universe[3] that's held together by powerful immaterial forces, like gravity and electromagnetism. It's a universe where the building blocks of physicality are wild and unpredictable atoms; atoms which themselves contain very little material physicality; atoms which are swirling and frenzied relationships of energy.

The ultimate reality undergirding, holding and sustaining the universe is not a physical, tangible object. It – or rather, they, he or she – is dynamic movement; alive and animated

action; pure and pulsating.
Like flickering flames.
Or a rushing wind.
And a mighty, swirling cloud.
All ways that the invisible God chose to become visible and accessible. These images offer a grappling, grasping, tantalising glimpse into the divine.
A bit like 'Father.'
Or 'King.'
'Lord.'
'Saviour.'
Or 'Shepherd.'
On their own – or even together.
These names will always fall short.
Because crucially: God is infinite.
If our divine image is limited to a physical form then – no matter how powerful they are – we are envisioning a 'god,' not 'God.' In English, the astronomical, categorical difference between finite and infinite is as subtle as a switch from lowercase to upper.
Having fled from a culture cluttered with clearly defined, sculpted gods, Moses' worldview began to explode when he dared to ask for the name of the mysterious voice calling to him from flickering flames.
We write God's response as 'Y-H-W-H.'
With an 'a' and an 'e' sometimes inserted.
To make the name pronounceable.
To make the name: 'Yahweh.'
Our best grasp of the meaning is 'I am who I am.'
Or equally, 'I will be who I will be.'[4]
Because the infinite's chosen name defies definition.
It resists restrictions.

It eludes limitations.

Which is why, shortly before his death, Moses implored his fledgling nation not to craft gods *"of any shape, whether formed like a man or a woman, or like any animal,"* because they had seen *"no form... out of the fire."*[5] The reluctant revolutionary stressed this despite being told by Yahweh, *"I will... cover you with my hand until I have passed by. Then I will remove my hand and you will see my back; but my face must not be seen."*[6]

God's own intriguing use of anthropomorphism, describing himself in finite, physical, and very human terms, can be thought of as a theoretical or poetical incarnation; a glimpse, a nod, a foretaste, a fore-runner to the remarkable moment two millennia ago when the second person of Elohim took on flesh.

When the fullness of God dwelt within atoms.

When the infinite was born in finite form.

When relationship took on substance.

When a verb became a noun.

When Jesus became *"the image of the invisible God."*[7]

This was not a quick dip-of-the-toe into our physical world. This was not a get-in-and-get-out mission to rescue humans, to help them escape the horrors of physicality. Instead, standing in stark contrast, the immaterial God, who created a solid, material world, plans to make that solid, material world his home.

We must care for this precious, fragile world not just because it is the Creator's handiwork, but because God desires to live here. Elohim's ultimate aim, Elohim's ultimate ambition is to reside upon a rescued, redeemed, repaired and restored earth.[8]

A recreated earth.

Logically a finite form cannot become infinite; but it is entirely possible and plausible for the infinite to fill and infuse the finite. So whereas Jesus walked alongside us – touching and embracing – the breath of Ruach can now pulsate inside of us, intimately indwelling. With Ruach within us, we become a visible and tangible body for the invisible, immaterial God.

This is the ultimate affirmation.

Of physicality's fundamental goodness.[9]

And when all things are made new.[10]

God will dwell among the rivers.

The trees.[11]

The crops.

The creatures.[12]

And a city of human constructions.[13]

This physical planet, filled with physical humans, will be the home address of the beyond-physical God.

Infinite: Beyond Physicality

1. Mark 14:36
2. Genesis 1:26
3. Colossians 1:16
4. Exodus 3:14
5. Deuteronomy 4:15-17
6. Exodus 33:22-23
7. Colossians 1:15
8. Revelation 21:3
9. Genesis 1:31
10. Revelation 21:5
11. Revelation 22:1
12. Isaiah 65:25
13. Isaiah 65:2

God is Infinite: Pouring Out

Since the beginning of time, our unfathomably enormous universe – of which we are yet to find an end – has been continuously expanding, pointing beyond itself to the outreaching, expanding, extroverted heart of its infinite origin; its perpetual maker. Only an infinite source can endlessly pour outwards without being diminished; without becoming less; without needing to be replenished or recharged. The boundless infinite God poured out a bounded finite creation, then rhetorically declared, *"Do not I fill heaven and earth?"*[1]
So we look around and wonder: really?
How?
Where?
Snapping from a dramatic dream under a star-lit night, Jacob's heart raced. Lifting his sore head from a rock, feeling the soil and vegetation between his fingers, the runaway fraudster uttered with astonished, awestruck eyes, *"Surely God is in this place, and I did not know it."*[2]
So we look around and wonder: really?
How?
Where?
Immersed within the mighty swirling cloud of Yahweh's unmistakable presence, King Solomon's heart soared with unadulterated joy, climactically cheering, *"Heaven and the highest heaven can not contain you."*[3] Similarly, his father David was overwhelmed by Elohim's immeasurable immensity, asking in awe, *"Where can I flee from your presence?"*[4]

So we look around and wonder: really?
How?
Where?
This is our challenge, our invitation: to tune, to heighten, to awaken our senses to the God who is already all around us, surrounding us, hemming us in, *"behind and before."*[5] So we look around and wonder: who or what and where is an invisible yet omnipresent God?

To begin our exploration, the Gospel-author John offers three clear and unequivocal answers.

"God is love."[6]

"God is light."[7]

"God is spirit"[8] – the original word also means breath and wind.

There are no poetical metaphors here. No similes.

John doesn't say, "God is like...."

He unerringly states: "God is...."

Which begs the question: if God is love, is love God? Should every loving act – or every ray from the sun, or every breath – be called 'God'? In mathematical logic A=B necessitates B=A. But that is not the case here. Alongside 'God is love,' John also wrote, *"Love comes from God."*[9]

Likewise, we can say: God is light and light comes from God; God is breath and breath comes from God.

Which means, the light, love and breath which surround us are all either God himself or – crucially – an overflow from God. As Elohim pours outwards, there is a point where love, light and breath leave God – and stop being God – and become a created entity of their own. Though they differ in their visibility and tangibility, the expansive and seemingly endless trio of love, light and breath are each absolutely central to life; and undoubtedly exist.

Even love: though we can't touch, taste, see, smell or hear it – though we can't measure or analyse it – we feel it, sense it at a deep inner level.
It drives us.
We need it.
We crave it.
God can move – intermingle – within the love, light and air around us because God is love, light and air. The God who is separate and distinct is also intimately close, surrounding us.
In the love that permeates and connects.
In the soothing solar light.
In the air we breathe.
To heighten awareness of the outward-looking, outward-pouring Elohim, the descendants of Abraham were encouraged to pour out drink,[10] oil[11] and blood offerings.[12] While, more dramatically, oil was poured over priests to commission their work.[13]
Blessed to be a blessing,[14] the Israelites were tasked with sharing the goodness they had enjoyed, pouring outwards to others, following and honouring their divine image.
Too often though, they turned inwards.
Prioritising selfish gain.
Neglecting.
Rejecting.
Or simply forgetting their call.
Conflicting and corroding their divine image.
In response, Abba, Yeshua and Ruach repeatedly promised that they would 'pour out' two contrasting things: to Isaiah,[15] Joel[16] and Ezekiel,[17] the embracing Elohim cheered with anticipatory delight, *"I will pour out my Spirit"*; while to Jeremiah,[18] Zephaniah,[19] Hosea[20] and Ezekiel,[21] they uttered

with anticipatory pain, *"I will pour out my wrath."*
Spirit.
And wrath.
At first glance, the pair appear to be equals, like two competing heavyweights. But there is a crucial, categorical difference: God's spirit is infinite, while God's wrath is finite. Wrath, grief and fury are a consequence; a reaction, a response. Before the first rebellion – before the first sin – there was no pain, no grief, no wrath within the complete and utter intimacy of Yeshua, Ruach and Abba.
Wrath had a beginning, and an end.
Wrath is time-limited; time-constrained.
When Daniel reflected upon the Judeans' devastating destruction and exile in Babylon, he understood, *"The curses and sworn judgments written in the Law of Moses… have been poured out on us, because we have sinned."*[22] Simultaneously, Daniel also knew that due to Yahweh's *"everlasting love"* and *"unfailing kindness"* there would be a joyous return from exile, with an abundant restoration of Judah.[23]
But by the time the Romans rolled in to rule, restoration and abundance had stalled and stagnated, leaving the Judeans fearful and bewildered. Stepping into this fog, fully human and finite, it became possible for the second person of Elohim to become drained and diminished. On a daily basis, Jesus needed replenishing.
He needed sleep.
He needed food.
And it became possible to empty himself fully.
Raising a glass of wine, Jesus announced, *"This is my blood of the covenant, which is poured out for many for the forgiveness of sins."*[24] Then the next day, as blood trickled and surged from his tortured body, Jesus quoted an agonising psalm which

includes the cry, *"I am poured out like water."*[25] Before Jesus breathed *"his last,"*[26] and *"poured out his life unto death... for he bore the sin of many."*[27]

Jesus' blood saves us, spares us, from the monumental, terrifying, deadly wrath of God.[28] All past, present and future wrath was fully absorbed, entirely deflected, redirected onto Jesus suspended on the cross, poured out upon him until there was none left.

Because love and light and breath pour out from Elohim endlessly, infinitely; but wrath poured out fully, once and for all, until there was no wrath left.

For God is love and light and spirit; and a myriad more.

But God is not wrath.

So now, instead of suffocating wrath heaped upon us, *"God gives the Spirit without limit,"*[29] with Ruach *"poured out on us generously,"*[30] rushing inside of us, soaring, flickering; inspiring, equipping and energising.[31] Like Yeshua before her, Ruach steps out with open arms for the purpose of pulling us into Elohim's euphoric, electrifying embrace.

"As the Father sent me," Jesus revealed, *"I am sending you."*[32] Which is why Paul repeatedly prayed that those indwelled by Ruach would themselves overflow.

Emitting love[33] and hope.[34]

Emanating joy and generosity.[35]

Radiating thanksgiving.[36]

Ushering others into Elohim's outstretched arms.

Sharing and spreading their divine message.

Following and honouring their divine image.

As we pour out and become diminished – tired and exhausted – Ruach wants to be the relentlessly replenishing source of our energy.

Our thoughts and words.

Our motivation and emotions.
Our mental health and self-worth.
United with the infinite, Elohim's unending, everlasting life erupts within us.[37] Forever, we will feast and flourish within the *"overflowing abundance"*[38] of the new creation, thoroughly sustained and immersed by the fullness of Love and Light and Spirit.

Infinite: Pouring Out

1. Jeremiah 23:24
2. Genesis 28:16
3. 1 Kings 8:27
4. Psalm 139:6
5. Psalm 139:4
6. 1 John 4:8
7. 1 John 1:5
8. John 4:24
9. 1 John 4:7
10. 2 Kings 16:13
11. Genesis 35:14
12. Leviticus 9:9
13. Exodus 19:7
14. Genesis 12:2
15. Isaiah 44:3
16. Joel 2:28
17. Ezekiel 39:29
18. Jeremiah 7:20
19. Zephaniah 3:8
20. Hosea 5:10
21. Ezekiel 20:13
22. Daniel 9:11
23. Jeremiah 31:3-5
24. Matthew 26:28
25. Psalm 22:14
26. Luke 23:46
27. Isaiah 53:12
28. Romans 5:9
29. John 3:34
30. Titus 3:5-6
31. Acts 2:2-4
32. John 20:21
33. 1 Thessalonians 3:12
34. Romans 15:13
35. 2 Corinthians 8:2
36. 2 Corinthians 4:15
37. John 10:27-28
38. Isaiah 66:11

"God Is..."

God is Love

The embracing community of Elohim is the very essence of Love. Abba, Yeshua and Ruach: they are Love itself. The individual persons of Father, Son and Holy Spirit are so intimately enveloped that they are one – they lovingly permeate one another so thoroughly, so absolutely that they constitute a single entity; a single being.
Abba, Ruach and Yeshua do not need anything or anyone to make them complete. The immersive trio love from a position of being perfectly, intimately, fully loved; knowing that they are precious, treasured and desired.
God loves because God is fully loved.
And the love of Abba, Yeshua and Ruach isn't just full to the brim.
It is brimming over.
Pouring out.
Bursting.
Exploding.
Like a fountain.
Or a *"spring of living water."*[1]
Love flows outwards, searching, reaching.
Rushing towards us with open arms.
The entire Biblical narrative is testament to this. Following a joyous outpouring of creation, Elohim sought out Abraham and fully committed, promising abundance and blessing. Then *"unfailing love"*[2] reached out and rescued, carrying his *"treasured possession"*[3] *"on eagles' wings."*[4] In a lush and lavish land, expanding and flourishing, King Solomon

praised the God who keeps his *"covenant of love"*;[5] whose *"love endures forever."*[6] Even the visiting Queen of Sheba acknowledged the God of Israel's *"eternal love."*[7]

"I am a *compassionate and gracious God,"* Love announced, *"slow to anger, abounding in love and faithfulness."*[8]

Yet when faced with repeated unfaithfulness.

Rejection.

Repulsion.

Affairs.

And incessant infidelity.

The enveloping Lovers of Elohim grieved.

Wept.

Desolate and heartbroken.

And the pain-stricken, long-suffering conclusion of slow-to-anger Love was devastating: *"I will give the one I love into the hands of her enemies."*[9]

Yet somehow, from the midst of utter destruction – caked in dust and dirt, surrounded by bloodied carcasses – somehow, a remarkable rasping cry arose: *"Because of Yahweh's great love we are not consumed, for his compassions never fail."*[10]

The heartbeat of Love hadn't stopped. The heartbeat of Love continued to pound as fervently as ever.

To Hosea, Love urged, *"Return."*[11]

To Isaiah: *"Return to me."*[12]

To Zechariah: *"Return to me… and I will return to you."*[13]

To Joel: *"Return to me with all your heart."*[14]

To Jeremiah: *"Return to me.*[15] For *I have loved you with an everlasting love… I will build you up again."*[16]

From the depths of their guts, the embracing Elohim cried: *"With deep compassion I will bring you back. In a surge of anger I hid my face from you for a moment, but with everlasting kindness I will have compassion on you... my unfailing love for you will not be shaken."*[17]

Because grace, forgiveness, mercy, compassion – everlasting kindness – they are the natural overflow of Love's surging heart. John's declaration that 'God is love' is not a sudden plot twist or a grand reveal. It is a majestic crescendo after millennia of passionate pursuit, encapsulating a heartbeat of an extrovert God who relentlessly loves outwardly.

Wooing.
Courting.
Romancing.
Imploring all: *"come close to me."*[18]
Then – making the first move – Love came close to us. Residing with his heart's desire, Jesus illustrated and demonstrated Elohim's gushing heart by endlessly reaching out, touching and embracing. Again and again, Jesus responded to teeming crowds with 'splagchnizomai' – a wonderful Greek word for an intense inward compassion felt in the depths of the guts or bowels.

Splagchnizomai is the word Jesus chose to describe a Samaritan nursing the wounds of a battered 'nemesis,'[19] and the heart of an estranged father searching and rushing and running with reaching, reuniting arms.[20]

Splagchnizomai is the word used to describe Jesus' compassion when he meets a grieving mother;[21] when he heals the sick,[22] restores sight[23] and provides a feast for the hungry.[24]

Jesus' inward emotion was consistently coupled with outward action.

Jesus was Love in person.
Love in action.
Love displayed.

Love made clear.

John wrote: *"This is how God showed his love among us: He sent his one and only Son into the world that we might live through him. This is love: not that we loved God, but that he loved us and sent his Son as an atoning sacrifice for our sins."*[25]

Because everything about Jesus, from his birth to his life to his death and resurrection, announced that every sinew of ultimate reality is lavish, generous, passionate Love.

We love because we are created by Love – in the image of Love. Mirroring the love between Abba, Yeshua and Ruach, we love others best from a position of loving ourselves; liking and accepting.

Our love ebbs and flows, oscillating between varying degrees of selfishness and selflessness; while ultimate Love is resolute and steadfast, always protecting, always trusting, always hoping, always persevering, never failing.[26]

Pure, perfect, pulsating Love not only draws alongside, but moves within and amongst, our faltering and flickering love – subtly and tenderly, often anonymously – for the purpose of pulling us forward into greater and brighter love. As we grow and mature and commit and work and teach and take on responsibilities, our focus moves beyond ourselves to others.

We become more like Jesus.

Our love becomes more like God's love.

"No one has ever seen God," John wrote, *"but if we love one another, God lives in us and his love is made complete in us."*[27]

With Love living within us, our fragile love becomes thoroughly overwhelmed and submerged – and transformed.

This is possible due to the continuing overflow of God.

Yeshua poured out from Abba to make Abba known.

And Ruach proceeded from Yeshua to make Yeshua known. And then we are commissioned, sent out, invited and instructed to continue the external flow, to reach outwards and reveal the love of Abba, Yeshua and Ruach to those around us.

Jesus said, *"As the Father has loved me, I have loved you."*[28]

And also, *"As I have loved you, so you must love one another."*[29]

This is the unending relay of love.

Flowing on back and forth.

Love inspires love.

In the image of Elohim – drawing from an infinite, endlessly replenishing source – we can love in the knowledge that we are intensely, passionately loved;[30] that we are precious and treasured and desired.

Love

1. Jeremiah 17:13
2. Exodus 15:13
3. Exodus 19:5
4. Exodus 19:4
5. 1 Kings 8:22
6. 2 Chronicles 7:3
7. 1 Kings 10:9
8. Exodus 34:6
9. Jeremiah 12:7
10. Lamentations 3:22
11. Hosea 14:1
12. Isaiah 44:22
13. Zechariah 1:3
14. Joel 2:12
15. Jeremiah 4:1
16. Jeremiah 31:3
17. Isaiah 54:5-10
18. Jeremiah 30:21
19. Luke 10:33
20. Luke 15:20
21. Luke 7:13
22. Matthew 14:14
23. Matthew 20:34
24. Matthew 15:32
25. 1 John 4:9-10
26. 1 Corinthians 13:7-8
27. 1 John 4:12
28. John 15:9
29. John 13:34
30. 1 John 4:19

God is Breath

In the aftermath of an almighty explosion, the divine breath hovered[1] over the scattered chaos, poised like an eagle, ready to craft and sculpt. Dynamic Ruach gathered the particles, crashing rocks through the darkness until beautiful spheres hung untethered across a multitude of galaxies.

Ruach's energy sprouted the seeds of nature, painting a panorama of wild colours; and then she blew her *"breath of life,"* animating a plethora of living creatures.[2]

Every second of every day since, the invigorating and pulsating Breath of Life has continued to exhilarate, revitalise and sustain the lavish earth and every living being.

In Ruach's world there is a mutual dependence – a collaboration – between creatures and vegetation, with each expiring the carbon dioxide or oxygen inhaled by the other.

There is also a mysterious connection – or fluidity – between wind and Spirit, with Jesus using the same word for both.[3] Likewise, in Ezekiel's evocative vision of dry bones rising to life, the word 'ruah' is used throughout, yet translations opt for 'Spirit,' 'breath' and 'winds,' depending on the context.[4]

Job was told, *"If God withdrew his spirit and breath, all humanity would perish together and mankind would return to the dust."*[5] And the wise counsel in Ecclesiastes taught that *"the dust returns to the ground it came from, and the spirit returns to God who gave it."*[6]

Because our every breath is a gift.
Poured out.
Breathed out.
Overflowing from God.
Even when Ruach's presence was rendered incompatible with humanity's near-universal violence and suffering,[7] the Breath of Life promised to sustain and animate our otherwise static physicality for up to 120 years.[8]
So there is breath that is from God: abundant and generous, yet limited in longevity. And then there is breath that is God: limitless and infinite.
When Moses stood stunned and aghast, reaching for breath on a dry, dusty plain, he requested the name of the God who had commissioned him to liberate slaves.
The fugitive murderer received four letters in reply.[9]
To modern eyes Y-H-W-H looks like four consonants.
But it's really four vowel sounds.
Four breathing sounds.
Ooh.
Heh.
Veh.
Heh.
Breathe it in and breathe it out.
Ooh.
Heh.
Veh.
Heh.
The name of God sounds like breathing.
Ooh.
Heh.
Veh.
Heh.

"I will put my Spirit in you."[10]
Ooh.
Heh.
Veh.
Heh.
God breathes in and God breathes out.
Ooh.
Heh.
Veh.
Heh.
Whether they realised it or not, Moses' liberated Israelites had the *"Holy Spirit among them."*[11] Bezalel and Oholiab, for example, were filled with an additional spirit, equipping them to construct and craft the tabernacle, a space to house the presence of God.[12]
Ruach danced at their creativity.
At the sharing of her divine artistry.
"The Spirit of the Lord will come powerfully upon you," Israel's first King was told, *"and you will be changed into a different person."*[13] But Saul's subsequent disobedience meant that Ruach *"departed from Saul"* and instead *"came powerfully upon David."*[14]
Showing Ruach brings the will, the heart, the desires of God, but she cannot guarantee obedience.
Then there were the prophets of Israel.
Ezekiel asserted, *"The Spirit came into me."*[15]
Micah: *"I am filled with power, with the Spirit of* Yahweh.*"*[16]
Isaiah: *"*Yahweh *has sent me, endowed with his Spirit."*[17]
This empowering and inspiring of key individuals was just a start, a taste, a glimpse of what was to come. Moses once angrily snapped, *"I wish that all* of Yahweh's *people were prophets and that* Yahweh *would put his Spirit on them!"*[18] And

sure enough, centuries later, the ecstatic embracing Elohim joyously proclaimed, "*I will pour out my Spirit on all people.*"[19] This prophecy was used to explain the frenzied explosion of new life[20] after the resurrected Jesus breathed upon his followers *and said, "Receive the Holy Spirit."*[21]
Ooh.
Heh.
Veh.
Heh.
With Ruach within us, we become the tabernacle, the home of the divine.[22] We become intimately united in relationship with the relational Trinity. The same Holy Spirit who so absolutely and intimately wraps around and permeates Father and Son, also lives in us. The outward-looking, outward-reaching Elohim stretches out their arms and pulls us close; wrapping around and dancing within.
Ooh.
Heh.
Veh.
Heh.
With Ruach within us, we become united to Yeshua who in turn unites us to Abba. We breathe in and receive the unblemished beauty of the one who was the ultimate marriage of spirit and matter, of the one who gave up his breath on a tree cut off from its source; whose limp, spiritless body was buried in the earth.
Ooh.
Heh.
Veh.
Heh.
With Ruach within us, we *"participate in the divine nature."*[23] We can breathe in and absorb the character of Elohim. Like

nature, we grow when we are rooted; connected; not cut off. As Jesus said, *"If you remain in me and I in you, you will bear much fruit."*[24]
Ooh.
Heh.
Veh.
Heh.
With Ruach within us, we can breathe out God's character to the world around us: love, joy, peace, patience, kindness, goodness, faithfulness, gentleness and self-control.[25] We are transformed into inspired co-creators, collaborators, joining with Ruach in the healing and re-creation of the world.[26]
Ooh.
Heh.
Veh.
Heh.
With Ruach within us, we too receive resurrection as our finite bodies become reconnected with their infinite source.
Ooh.
Heh.
Veh.
Heh.
With Ruach within us, God is right under our nose.
God is in our nostrils.[27]
In our lungs.
In our inhaling and exhaling.
We breathe God in and breathe God out.

Breath

1. Genesis 1:2
2. Genesis 1:30
3. John 3:8
4. Ezekiel 37:1-14
5. Job 34:14-15
6. Ecclesiastes 12:7
7. Genesis 6:5
8. Genesis 6:3
9. Exodus 3:14
10. Ezekiel 36:25-27
11. Isaiah 63:11
12. Exodus 35:31-33
13. 1 Samuel 10:6
14. 1 Samuel 16:13-14
15. Ezekiel 2:2
16. Micah 3:8
17. Isaiah 48:16
18. Numbers 11:29
19. Joel 2:28
20. Acts 2:16
21. John 20:22
22. 1 Peter 2:5
23. 2 Peter 1:4
24. John 15:5
25. Galatians 5:22-23
26. Isaiah 32:15
27. Job 27:3-4

God is Light

In the beginning, Light created light.

The first extroverted creative command of Uncreated Light was to say to the darkness, *"Let there be light."*[1] And in a flash, out of nothing, there were photons, flooding the universe with light. The very first light in the universe was beyond the visible range of a human eye yet its intensity would have burned our eyes in an instant.

Then, on the fourth day of creation – roughly 4.6 billion years ago, when the universe was already 9.2 billion years old – a cloud of dust and gas collapsed in on itself as the incandescent Elohim placed a sphere of hot plasma at the centre of a new solar system. The star – our sun – comprises 99.86% of the solar system's mass. It is heated by nuclear fusion reactions, and releases energy as visible light and many other invisible frequencies of photons. Moving mysteriously with wave-particle duality, light takes just 8.5 minutes to travel nearly 100 million miles from the sun to earth.

It is the *"light of life."*[2]

Animating.

Energising.

And sustaining.

Every living thing.

Perfectly positioned and proportioned for life on earth to flourish, our sun emits light and heat purely because it is light and heat. And in a similar way, created, measurable light overflowed from Elohim's uncreated, immeasurable

embrace, purely because Elohim is light.
"*Light dwells with* God,"[3] Daniel declared.
"*You are radiant with light,*"[4] Asaph eulogised.
"*Yahweh wraps himself in light,*"[5] adds an anonymous Psalm.
"*Let the light of your face shine on us,*"[6] David petitioned, before later proclaiming, "*out of the brightness of his presence bolts of lightning blazed forth.*"[7] Similarly, in his "*visions of God,*"[8] Ezekiel saw "*an immense cloud with flashing lightning and surrounded by brilliant light.*"[9]
When Moses spoke "*face to face*" with God,[10] uncreated light became visible within creation, causing the revolutionary's face to reflect and radiate such searing luminosity that it was dangerous for others to look at him.[11] When Saul – later Paul – was immersed by an almighty explosion of divine light, he described its intensity as "*brighter than the sun.*"[12]
At Jesus' transfiguration, John witnessed Jesus' face shine "*like the sun,*" and his clothes become "*as white as the light.*"[13] John went on to eloquently explain, "*The true light that gives light to everyone was coming into the world.*"[14] He then quoted Jesus imploring, "*Believe in the light while you have the light, so that you may become children of light.*"[15]
It all led John to his startling, epic conclusion: Jesus could, quite literally, claim, "*I am the light of the world*"[16] because God is light. But when Jesus also declared to his followers, "*you are the light of the world,*" instructing them to "*shine before others,*"[17] he clearly wasn't implying that they would replace the role of the sun. Instead, this was Jesus' invitation to continue Israel's mission to be a light to their neighbours.[18]
To radiate the divine image.
Reflecting God's goodness.
Refracting God's character.

Invigorating and energising.
Illuminating and enlightening.
Because light enables us to see.
Light exposes *"what is hidden in darkness."*[19]
Light forces vulnerability and honesty and openness.
And in the Community of Elohim everything is open, everything is shared, everything is known. Between Abba, Yeshua and Ruach there is full exposure; all are fully vulnerable; nothing is hidden. For *"God is light and in him there is no darkness."*[20]
So when we confess – when we shine light on our hidden darkness – we are becoming more like the divine; more like the light who created us in his image.
"Yahweh *is my light,"* David sang.[21]
"Let us walk in the light of Yahweh," Isaiah instructed.[22]
"Though I sit in darkness," Micah wrote, "Yahweh *will be my light… He will bring me out into the light."*[23]
God's metaphorical light can flood humanity's metaphorical darkness.
During the exodus from Egypt, the Egyptians were literally plunged into darkness for three days, while intermingling Israelites – remarkably – enjoyed sunlight as normal.[24] Uncreated Light exhibited precise control over created light. And subsequently, in the process, darkness became synonymous with judgement and punishment.
"Why do you long for the day of the Lord?" Yahweh asked. *"That day will be darkness, not light."*[25] *"When I snuff you out, I will cover the heavens and darken their stars; I will cover the sun with a cloud, and the moon will not give its light."*[26] Likewise, Yahweh warned Isaiah of *"a cruel day, with wrath and fierce anger"* when *"the stars of heaven and their constellations will not show their light."*[27]

Jesus referenced these warnings shortly before his death[28] but added that his subsequent victory would, *"be like the lightning, which flashes and lights up the sky from one end to the other."*[29]

And sure enough, as Jesus hung in excruciating agony – for three torturous hours in the middle of the day – *"the sun stopped shining"* and *"darkness came over the whole land."*[30]

Then for two nights, Jesus' dead body lay buried, encased in darkness.

Before supernatural light *"like lightning."*[31]

Gleamed.

And flashed.

And blazed.

Jesus absorbed the full darkness of judgement.

Jesus defeated the powers of darkness.

But Jesus also brought about the end of darkness, full stop.

Because in both Isaiah and John's visions of a restored heaven and earth, each saw a future where the earth no longer spins around the sun; where day no longer turns to night; where light never fails to shine.[32]

"For the glory of God gives it light."[33]

John even heard Jesus describe himself as *"the bright Morning Star"*[34] and saw Jesus' face *"like the sun shining in all its brilliance."*[35]

So the next time we bathe in the sun's rays, or observe a plant reaching towards sunlight, we are not just appreciating light created by Light, we are also enjoying a glimmer of a new era when humanity will live thoroughly immersed within divine radiance, basking in Elohim's *"everlasting light."*[36]

Endlessly energised and animated.

By the ultimate Light of Life.[37]

Light

1. Genesis 1:3
2. Psalm 49:19
3. Daniel 2:22
4. Psalm 76:4
5. Psalm 104:2
6. Psalm 4:6
7. 2 Samuel 22:13
8. Ezekiel 1:1
9. Ezekiel 1:4
10. Exodus 33:11
11. Exodus 34:34-35
12. Acts 26:13
13. Matthew 17:1-2
14. John 1:9
15. John 12:36
16. John 8:12
17. Matthew 5:14-16
18. Isaiah 49:6
19. 1 Corinthians 4:5
20. 1 John 1:5
21. Psalm 27:1
22. Isaiah 2:5
23. Micah 7:8-9
24. Exodus 10:22-23
25. Amos 5:18
26. Ezekiel 32:7
27. Isaiah 13:9-10
28. Matthew 24:29
29. Luke 17:24
30. Luke 27:44-45
31. Luke 24:4
32. Revelation 22:5
33. Revelation 21:23
34. Revelation 22:16
35. Revelation 1:16
36. Isaiah 60:19
37. John 8:12

Relationship

God is Relationship: Community

The definitive reality underpinning and permeating throughout and beyond the cosmos is a relationship of persons; the interweaving and overlapping unbreakable bond between Father, Son and Holy Spirit.
No one person in the Trinity is lesser, lonely or lacking. Elohim's encircling embrace is not a hierarchical triangle with one on top, lording over two subsidiary agents. The lovers did not create out of need or jealousy or a human-shaped hole in their heart. Instead, fully satisfied, fully known and fully loved, they gave birth to the universe out of the pounding, passionate desire of their overflowing heart. The Community of Elohim created humans in kind as relational beings, offering union with their ultimate union, and desiring the growth of human communities in their loving image.
Differentiation without discrimination.
Diversity within unity.
And unity within diversity.
By contrast, solitary-yet-powerful gods are scary prospects.
Needy and greedy, they exacerbate inequalities.
Dictating and demanding, they validate tyranny.
Violent and vengeful, they perpetuate bloodshed.
These widespread, deeply rooted and deeply disturbing misconceptions played a part in plunging primitive human societies down to the darkest depths of depravity. With violence and bloodshed normalised and commonplace, *"every inclination of the thoughts of the human heart was only evil all the time."*[1]

Grieved throughout their heart and captivated by a single ray of hope,[2] Abba, Yeshua and Ruach resolved to wholeheartedly commit to the cultivation of human societies. Beginning with the intimacy of lovers giving birth to a family,[3] Yahweh grew a nation to galvanise and revolutionise the world.

Rescued from slavery, new governing laws were presented to an emerging and fledgling society, aimed at organising and orienting, pulling humanity forwards towards a better divine resemblance. Not only did the new rules prohibit negative destructive behaviours[4] but they also actively promoted positive restorative actions.

Fair trade.[5]

Reconciliation.[6]

Rights for workers.[7]

Annual celebrations.[8]

Respect for the elderly.[9]

Protecting children from abuse.[10]

Restricting the spread of infection.[11]

Treating immigrants as *"native-born."*[12]

Plus, for those short of finances there was the promise of fair legal representation,[13] provision of necessities[14] and proportional affordability.[15]

This was kindness.

This was compassion.

But it was also justice; social justice.

King Solomon stressed, *"Whoever oppresses the poor shows contempt for their Maker, but whoever is kind to the needy honours God."*[16] And regarding Josiah's kingship, Yahweh explained, *"He defended the cause of the poor and the needy, and so it went well. Is that not what it means to know me?"*[17]

Stifling others defiles our divine image.

While helping others restores it.
Reaching out reflects the image of an outreaching God.
Again and again the Israelites were reminded: look after the marginalised and oppressed, because deep in the heart of your collective psyche you know what it is like to suffer as lesser through no fault of your own.[18]

However, as the nation of Israel prospered, the Community of Elohim witnessed their chosen people *"sell the innocent for silver"* and *"trample on the heads of the poor."*[19] The frustrated, exasperated trio repeatedly urged, *"If you really change your ways and deal with each other justly… and do not shed innocent blood… then I will let you live in this place."*[20]

But eventually – eventually – justice had to be done.

Because crimes require consequences.

"I will come to put you on trial," Yahweh announced, prosecuting and testifying against all *"who defraud labourers of their wages, who oppress the widows and the fatherless, and deprive the foreigners."*[21]

The one who is just,[22] who *"loves justice"*[23] and *"loves the just,"*[24] had ardently and fervently *"looked for justice, but saw bloodshed; for righteousness, but heard cries of distress."*[25]

So the city where the divine dwelt on earth became filled with bloodshed.[26]

And cries of distress.[27]

Haunted by his ancestors' failures, Nehemiah returned to the *"desolate waste"*[28] of Jerusalem's rubble and implemented radical social reforms. After meeting with poverty-stricken parents forced to sell their own children for funds,[29] Nehemiah swiftly removed the *"heavy burden"* of extortionate taxation.[30]

But by the time Jesus announced that he had come *"to set the oppressed free,"*[31] life in society's margins was as

harrowing as ever. Proclaiming the seed-like emergence of a new 'Kingdom' – a society in the image of God – Jesus gravitated to the 'lesser' and lonely and lacking without hesitation, smashing through social conventions and barriers as if they didn't exist.
Before surrendering himself to the very worst of humanity.
Crucifixion was anti-community.
Crucifixion was ruling through fear.
Crucifixion was maintaining a hierarchy.
Crucifixion was a society far, far, far from its divine image.
And hung *"outside the city gate,"*[32] Jesus suffered as a victim of injustice and an ostracised outcast, exiled from both his earthly community and – more shockingly – his heavenly community. For, having only ever known an eternal unshakable, unbreakable, inseparable bond with Abba and Ruach, Jesus roared in gut-wrenching fury and horror, sorrow and bewilderment, *"My God, my God, why have you forsaken me?"*[33]
Because with blood shed.
And a cosmic cry of distress.
The cross ripped at the heart of divine intimacy.
Temporarily tore apart the divine unity.
Sliced a schism in the divine community.
The fullness of God died as an outcast – from God.
Lesser.
Lonely.
And lacking.
Before resurrection.
Brought the exile home.
With the rapturous Ruach surrounding and infusing, Abba and Yeshua's collective heart soared with delight as they sent forth Ruach, rushing around and within a group of

Jesus' expectant followers, *"powerfully"* transforming them into an image of Elohim.
Where all were *"one in heart and mind."*[34]
Where no one was lesser.
Lonely.
Or lacking.[35]
In unison with Abba and Ruach, Jesus had vigorously prayed for his future followers to *"be one as we are one"*;[36] and while the idyllic image depicted by Luke didn't last long, it remains an aspirational snapshot of potential.
As the early church rapidly expanded, Paul spoke into the messy complexity of merging cultures, urging all to *"live in harmony,"*[37] stressing that all were *"one in Christ Jesus."*[38] Eroding prejudices, Ruach equips individuals with *"different gifts"*[39] for varying roles, all for the *"common good."*[40]
Paul also had to grapple with the extent to which Yahweh's laws – given one and a half millennia ago – still applied to a multinational community no longer *"under the law, but under grace."*[41] Fulfilled by Jesus,[42] some laws were now deemed obsolete, or regressive, while others remained progressive and restorative. What ultimately mattered was the spirit of the law governed by *"the law of the Spirit"*;[43] Ruach's inspiration of hearts and minds,[44] animating and invigorating our communal calling to mirror and communicate the communal God of differentiation without discrimination.
Of diversity within unity.
And unity within diversity.
So our every interaction matters.
The invisible relational bonds between us matter.
Because the Bible begins with the creative work of the divine community, and ends with the collaborative creative

work of human and divine. It begins with individuals commissioned to order and craft and sculpt the raw materials of the wild world before them. And it ends with a harmonious global community – a civilisation – in a city; the product of human hands working together and the home of the one who is the very nature and essence of Relationship, dwelling among and within the invisible relational bonds between us.

Relationship: Community

1. Genesis 6:5
2. Genesis 6:6-8
3. Genesis 21:2
4. Exodus 20:13-16
5. Leviticus 19:35-36
6. Leviticus 6:1-5
7. Exodus 23:12
8. Leviticus 23:3-8
9. Leviticus 19:32
10. Leviticus 20:4-5
11. Leviticus 13:5
12. Leviticus 19:34
13. Exodus 23:6
14. Exodus 23:11
15. Leviticus 5:7-11
16. Proverbs 14:31
17. Jeremiah 22:15
18. Deuteronomy 15:15
19. Amos 2:6-7
20. Jeremiah 7:5-7
21. Malachi 3:5
22. Deuteronomy 32:4
23. Psalm 99:4
24. Psalm 37:28
25. Isaiah 5:7
26. Lamentations 4:14
27. Lamentations 1:3
28. Ezekiel 33:29
29. Nehemiah 5:5-6
30. Nehemiah 5:15
31. Luke 4:18
32. Hebrews 13:12
33. Matthew 27:46
34. Acts 4:32
35. Acts 4:33
36. John 17:22
37. Romans 12:16
38. Galatians 3:28
39. Romans 12:6
40. 1 Corinthians 12:7
41. Romans 6:14
42. Matthew 5:17
43. Romans 8:2
44. Hebrews 10:15-16

God is Relationship: Family

From quantum quarks to ecological ecosystems, we're becoming increasingly aware of the interconnectivity of all things. The fundamental heart, the foundational essence of the created order is relationship – interdependency – bursting, surging from the uncreated Elohim; perpetually pulsing and emanating from Relationship themselves.
Sharing themselves with each other, committed couples imitate something of Elohim's passionate intimacy.
With naked honesty and vulnerability.
Taking on a collective identity.
Working collaboratively.
Sharing resources.
Putting a partner's needs ahead of their own.
No relationship is a perfect resemblance of Elohim's all-pervasive community, but they are a pale reflection: the two are one, and the one is two. And then in time of course, in many cases, the two become three. Out of love comes new life. And the couple begin to give themselves collectively to another.
Love expands.
Love pours over.
Creation was the explosive overflow from the complete and utter intimacy of divine lovers – our heavenly Father and Mother – giving birth to the earth and every animated being. And fashioned in Elohim's likeness, the intimacy of human lovers continues to populate and *"fill the earth."*[1]
Many, if not most, of humanity's deepest relational bonds

are familial; and in Elohim's tri-unity, there is Father and Son. Each finds their identity in relation to the other.
Abba is 'Father' because he has a Son.
And Yeshua is 'Son' because he has a Father.
There is an inextricable link; the deepest interdependency.
"The Father loves the Son."[2]
And the Son loves the Father.[3]
But the idea of God being a father didn't begin with Yeshua's incarnation. Moses asked the Israelites, *"Is he not your Father, your Creator?"*[4] While Malachi challenged, *"Do we not all have one Father? Did not one God create us?"*[5]
So 'Father' was used as a synonym for 'Creator.'
But Job stretched the metaphor further, seamlessly switching from enquiring, *"Does the rain have a father?"* to asking, *"From whose womb comes the ice?"*[6]
Because creation was conceived.
And carried.
Before being born.
Isaiah twice declared to Yahweh, *"You are our Father,"*[7] yet also heard Elohim compare her captivated heart to that of a breastfeeding mother,[8] gently and tenderly whispering, *"As a mother comforts her child, so will I comfort you."*[9] The line was strikingly reminiscent of King David's lyric: *"As a father has compassion on his children, so* Yahweh *has compassion"*;[10] and also Moses' reflective recollection: *"God carried you, as a father carries his son."*[11]
Comforting.
Compassionate.
And carrying.
Like Israel's surrounding nations, with their legions of gods, a divine Father-Son relationship was a privilege of their monarch.[12] But unlike Israel's surrounding nations, the

whole nation was also collectively entitled: Yahweh's *"firstborn son."*[13]

"I am Israel's father,"[14] Abba revealed, *"and my heart yearns for him."*[15] Yet with searing regret, Abba also lamented, *"I thought you would call me Father."*[16]

Here is Elohim's aching, breaking heart.

Longing to be known as Father.

"It was I who taught Ephraim to walk," Yahweh recalled. *"I led them with cords of human kindness, with ties of love. To them I was like one who lifts a little child to the cheek, and I bent down to feed them."*[17]

This is one of several passages which describe God's parental heart, without attributing a gender.

For, after all, God is beyond gender.

Our triune Father and Mother is neither biologically male or female. Through the incarnation Yeshua became male, but the male-heavy 'Father-Son' language used by Jesus does not imply that Abba is also male.

Fully-God and fully-human, Jesus was the complete and perfect intersection – the perfect embrace – of divine and human for the simple but staggeringly significant reason that he had a heavenly Father and a human Mother.

Mary had not been a surrogate carrier or adoptive parent for Jesus, as amazing as that still would have been. Jesus had Mary's DNA. Presumably, he inherited a physical likeness – family traits – but more importantly, this explains why Jesus never prayed to God as 'Mother.'

His Mother was Mary.

For the rest of us however, Abba, Ruach and Yeshua desperately, passionately – throughout the entirety of their infinite being – desire to be known as both Father and Mother.

So it's important to realise that when we describe God in 'Father-Son' terms, we are solely describing a relationship within Elohim's embrace, not Elohim's relationship with us. Jesus taught us to approach God as *"our Father,"*[18] but clearly God is not also 'our Son.'

'Father-Son-Spirit' is a description of Elohim's inward, internal relations.

'Father-Mother-Brother,' on the other hand, has been proposed as a way of capturing something of Elohim's outward relationships towards us.

In this approximation, Abba is our Father.

Ruach is our Mother.

And Jesus is our Brother.

Just as 'Father-Son' shouldn't suggest a male or masculine imbalance in God, it also shouldn't subtly sow a misconception that Yeshua is younger than Abba, or less mature. The Father generated – or begat – the Son outside of time. So Father and Son are both beyond age; neither had a beginning. Abba is not training or educating – or disciplining – Yeshua. God the Son is equally as powerful as God the Father, so *"whatever the Father does the Son also does."*[19]

By contrast, the dynamic of human parent-child relationships can vary considerably, fluctuating from the care given by a parent at the beginning of a child's life, all the way through to the care given by offspring at the end of a parent's life.

Combining the images offers a slight glimpse into the perfectly consistent, mutual dependency of Abba and Yeshua, whose utmost care for each other is unchanging, unaffected by age.

So when the New Testament depicts Jesus as *"appointed heir of all things,"*[20] it is describing an inheritance unlike any other; an inheritance received, not after the death of his father.

But after the death of himself.

Watching Jesus hang desolately, Mary wept and wailed as her own flesh and blood had his flesh and blood ripped and shredded and drained. Staring at her suspended son in sheer, absolute, helpless horror, grieving the death of her firstborn,[21] Mary's torture would have been the visual representation of Abba's own unimaginable, immeasurable agony.

Grieving the death of his firstborn.

Mourning the loss of his one and only.

On behalf of us all, Yeshua became the ultimate prodigal far from home; before resurrection returned the Son to his Father's ecstatic, euphoric – sprinting and stretching – reuniting embrace.

Likewise, we can also imagine the most wonderful tears of joy filling the sensational reunion embrace of Jesus with his Mother Mary. It's intriguing to speculate why we have no record of the event; perhaps the moment was just too private?

Too personal?

Too precious to share?

In John's meticulously constructed gospel, packed with theological symbolism, Jesus refers to 'my Father' or 'the Father' on over one hundred occasions. But post-resurrection, there's a sudden significant shift when Jesus instructs Mary Magdalene, "Go *to my brothers, and tell them, 'I am ascending to my Father and your Father.'*"[22]

Expanding and expounding this idea, Paul wrote, "*Because you are his sons, God sent the Spirit of his Son into our hearts, the Spirit who calls out, 'Abba, Father.'"*[23] *"The Spirit you received brought about your adoption to sonship. And by him we cry, 'Abba, Father.'"*[24]

Through Jesus' most excruciating labour – naked and gasping and covered in blood – we can *"become children of God."*[25]

Through Jesus, our brother, we too can call God 'Abba.'

We become *"co-heirs"* of Jesus' cosmic inheritance.[26]

Invited – adopted – into the family of God.

Relationship: Family

1. Genesis 1:28
2. John 3:35
3. John 14:31
4. Deuteronomy 32:6
5. Malachi 2:10
6. Job 38:28-29
7. Isaiah 63:16
8. Isaiah 49:15
9. Isaiah 66:13
10. Psalm 103:13
11. Deuteronomy 1:31
12. Psalm 2:7
13. Exodus 4:22
14. Jeremiah 31:9
15. Jeremiah 31:20
16. Jeremiah 3:19
17. Hosea 11:1-4
18. Matthew 6:9
19. John 5:19
20. Hebrews 1:1
21. John 19:26
22. John 20:17
23. Galatians 4:6
24. Romans 8:15
25. John 1:12
26. Romans 8:17

God is Relationship: Lover

Flowing back and forth between all things, binding and bonding, Love is not merely an invisible force or an intangible power; a mysterious, unexaminable entity or substance. The God who is Love is a being – a person – who actively, dynamically, relentlessly loves.
Love loves.
Love is a passionate lover.
Three persons all-in-all, the lovers of Elohim are totally besotted and devoted, both inwardly and outwardly.
Abba is the beloved of Ruach and Yeshua.
Yeshua is the beloved of Abba and Ruach.
Ruach is the beloved of Yeshua and Abba.
And we are the beloved of all three.
Elohim's adoring, joyful inner union is the most pure and straightforward love story – entirely and thoroughly faithful – completely, consistently awash with mutual, reciprocal affection.
Love's outward relationship with humanity, however, has been anything but simple. That story has been a rocky, up-and-down, on-and-off saga, riddled by unrequited love. It's a story of a one-sided passionate pursuit, wooing, romancing, eagerly seeking response, desiring the emergence of an intimate two-way relationship.
When humans are involved, response is never certain; reciprocation is never guaranteed. When we reach out, when we put our heart on the line, we risk crushing heartbreak for the possibility of exhilarating joy.

And we do so in the image of Elohim.
Because to love is to take a chance.
To choose.
And commit.
Again and again.
Intently and relentlessly.
Decisively and tenaciously, through thick and thin.
Ruach, Abba and Yeshua's initial interactions with Abraham and his offspring introduced the Community of Elohim's intimate intentions, while the Egyptian exodus was Love's great gesture of courtship; a demonstrative display of desire and affection.
In response, the Israelites said *"we will"* to covenanting their union and allegiance with Yahweh, committing to exclusivity and fidelity with the exchanging of vows.[1]
"You shall have no other gods before me,"[2] Israel's Groom demanded. And for a brief moment, in the mountainous wilderness, there was intimacy.
Undivided attention.
Undefiled affection.
Undiluted, undisputed affiliation.
This was the Mount Sinai marriage ceremony.
Before the embryonic nation sculpted a statue like those in Egypt, and proclaimed, *"These are your gods, Israel, who brought you up out of Egypt."*[3]
The jilted Elohim didn't just feel jealous; Abba, Yeshua and Ruach's very name was Jealous.[4]
Because Love desires to be loved.
Elohim's heart aches when his affection is not reciprocated; when his heart's desire is looking elsewhere, flirting and fraternising with those who can offer nothing in return. Which is why, from the exodus onwards, Yahweh

frequently – and shockingly – described the pursuit of other gods as an act of prostitution.[5]

The most shallow relationship possible.

With no commitment.

No depth.

No heart.

Growing up in the desert, shielded from the lure of other gods, a new generation of Israelites entered their Promised Land without the entrenched habits of their parents, knowing that they were the *"apple of* Yahweh's *eye."*[6]

And for a brief moment, in their bountiful marital home, there was intimacy.

Unanimous association.[7]

Unadulterated appreciation.

Unambiguous, unabridged aspiration.

This was a belated honeymoon period.

Before successive generations *"prostituted themselves to other gods,"*[8] dismissing their doting Husband as if he didn't even exist.[9]

King David helped rekindle Israel's divine relationship, singing to Yahweh, *"My whole being longs for you,"*[10] alongside instructing his son and successor to build an earthly residence for Yahweh.

At the Temple's grand opening, surrounded by an exhilarating, visible, tangible divine presence,[11] King Solomon prayed for the blossoming of a faithful two-way divine-human relationship.[12]

And for a brief moment, in a flourishing Israel, there was intimacy.

Unrivalled adulation.

Unreserved adoration.

Unrestricted, unrestrained ambition.

Relationship: Lover

This was a recommitment; a vow renewal.
Before Solomon worshipped Ashtoreth.
And Chemosh.
And Molek.[13]
Initiating a chain of events[14] which led to most of Israel relinquishing allegiance to the line of David.
Breaking away from Judah.
And by default: Yahweh.
Needing a new god, the revolutionaries built two golden calves and declared, "*Here are your gods, Israel, who brought you up out of Egypt.*"[15]
Through the prophets, Abba, Yeshua and Ruach poured out their pain.
Revealing a wounded, broken heart.
Overflowing with prevailing hope.
In the long term, through Isaiah, Love promised to transform the promiscuous prostitute into *"a crown of splendour."* No longer called 'Deserted' or 'Desolate,' they will be 'Delighted in'; their very name, very identity, would be 'Married.'[16] *"Your Maker is your husband,"*[17] Yahweh amorously declared. *"With deep compassion I will bring you back."*[18]
In the short term, however, the rejected romantic watched on through tumbling tears as his estranged beloved Israel was conquered and ravaged by the Assyrians.[19]
Through Jeremiah, the embracing Elohim shared precious memories of fleeting bridal affection,[20] before warning Judah, *"I gave faithless Israel her certificate of divorce and sent her away because of all her adulteries,"*[21] yet *"faithless Israel is more righteous than unfaithful Judah."*[22] *"Return, faithless people,"* Love cried, *"for I am your husband."*[23]
Through Ezekiel, the adoring Lovers recalled adorning their

bride with glamorous gifts, transforming her into a majestic queen[24] – who then used her beauty in pursuit of others. So, submitting to the will of his *"adulterous wife,"* Elohim howled, *"You prefer strangers to your own husband!"*[25]
Then left Judah alone in *"the hands of her lovers."*
Knowing full well that they would chew her up.
And spit her out.
And *"leave her stark naked."*[26]
Through Hosea, Yahweh communicated Israel and Judah's promiscuity in the most dramatic way possible, instructing the prophet to marry a prostitute and start a family – despite the overwhelming likelihood of his wife continuing to lie with clients.
Incessant infidelity was the reason God gave for forcing his dearly beloved out from the Promised Land and back into the wilderness; where – free from all distractions and temptations, alone again in their place of first love – they would be wooed.
And allured.[27]
To fall in love all over again.
"You will call me 'my husband,'"[28] Love vowed via Hosea, *"and I will betroth you to me forever."*[29] Captivated, Hosea was next told to return to his unfaithful wife and pay money for her attention.[30]
Which points us to Yeshua.
Paying the ultimate price.[31]
For his ultimate prize.
The apple of his eye.
His heart's desire.
Jesus surrendered himself to eradicate his beloved's every crushing infidelity, every poisonous promiscuity, every heartbreaking affair, *"to present her to himself as a radiant*

church, without stain or wrinkle or any other blemish."[32]
Depicting himself as *"the bridegroom,"*[33] Jesus' first miracle was at a wedding,[34] giving a glorious glimpse of an eternally abundant, endlessly satisfying *"wedding banquet."*[35]
To which everyone is invited.[36]
For which we should eagerly wait.
And attentively prepare for.[37]
Paul called Jesus our *"one husband,"*[38] while John vividly and evocatively foresaw the culmination – the consummation – of a new heaven and earth coming together in holy matrimony. *"The wedding of the Lamb has come,"* roared a thunderous congregation as John saw *"the bride, the wife of the Lamb,"*[39] clothed in pure dazzling white,[40] processing gracefully toward her besotted betrothed.
And like in the Song of Songs – the Bible's great celebration of passionate, pleasurable, sensual, sexual love – Husband and Wife will take turns to pour out infatuated words of romance.
Lost in each other's arms.
To have and to hold from this day forward.
There will be intimacy – with Intimacy.
With Love: the passionate Lover.

Relationship: Lover

1. Exodus 19:4-8
2. Exodus 20:3
3. Exodus 32:4
4. Exodus 34:14
5. Exodus 34:15-16
6. Deuteronomy 32:10
7. Joshua 24:16-18
8. Judges 2:17
9. Judges 8:33
10. Psalm 63:1
11. 1 Kings 8:10
12. 1 Kings 8:57-58
13. 1 Kings 11:5-8
14. 1 Kings 11:11-13
15. 1 Kings 12:28
16. Isaiah 62:3-5
17. Isaiah 54:5
18. Isaiah 54:7
19. 2 Kings 18:11-12
20. Jeremiah 2:2
21. Jeremiah 3:8
22. Jeremiah 3:11
23. Jeremiah 3:14
24. Ezekiel 16:11-13
25. Ezekiel 16:32
26. Ezekiel 16:39
27. Hosea 2:14
28. Hosea 2:16
29. Hosea 2:19
30. Hosea 3:2-3
31. 1 Corinthians 6:20
32. Ephesians 5:25-27
33. Matthew 9:15
34. John 2:9-11
35. Matthew 22:2
36. Matthew 22:8-10
37. Matthew 25:10
38. 2 Corinthians 11:2
39. Revelation 21:9
40. Revelation 7:14

Bliss

God is Bliss: Beauty

The greatest works of art possess extraordinary complexity and breathtaking simplicity. At first glance, there is elegant unity – a single, simple entity – but then, drawn in, we gaze in mesmerised wonder at layer upon layer of bewildering detail.
Like the unique exquisite symmetry of a snowflake.
Like the golden spiralling seeds of a sunflower.
Like a swarm of bees tessellating hexagons.
Like a flock of birds swooping in unison.
Like a twinkling, glistening diamond.
Throughout the created world – from the telescopic glimpse of a galactic nebula to the microscopic image of, well, practically anything – we see the phenomenon of beauty produced by the unity of diversity and multiplicity; immense complexity underpinning ultimate simplicity.
And taking this logic to its absolute extreme, we find Elohim.
We find Abba, Yeshua and Ruach.
A single unity with infinite complexity.
A perfect harmony composing a rapturous symphony.
Not the mere simplicity of three gods.
Or one God appearing in three forms.
But the beautiful simplicity and complexity of three persons, mutually indwelling. Or in the words of early church theologians: three persons with 'homoousion' in 'perichoresis.' 'Homoousion' stresses Abba, Yeshua and Ruach's one single identical essence or nature, while

'perichoresis' proclaims the energetic and dynamic synchronicity and perfect choreography of Elohim's all-encompassing, encircling embrace.

It's tempting to think that beauty is purely subjective. But beauty exists – beauty is here, right now, all around us – whether we notice it or not.

Like God, beauty has to be encountered first-hand.

Like God, beauty is waiting to be discovered.

Like God, beauty can endlessly astound.

Like God, beauty transcends purpose.

Beauty defies explanation.

Beauty just is.

There are so many parallels because all beauty in our lives is a gift exploding out from the gushing extroverted heart of Beauty herself. All beauty that we encounter is either God himself or beauty which has flowed out from God, pointing back to God.

David longed to *"gaze on the beauty of* Yahweh,"[1] while Asaph sang, *"From Zion, perfect in beauty, God shines forth."*[2] For the one who sculpts and crafts and animates the dust is the one who enables us to encounter raw materials and sense something more. Ruach both resides within beauty and connects us to beauty, enlivening our heart, exhilarating our spirit, drawing our inner, invisible being closer to the ultimate Beauty who existed before – and continues to exist beyond – all visibility and tangibility.

Because creation was beauty becoming visible.

Creation was beauty taking shape, taking form.

And we were – we are – the heart, the pinnacle.

Beauty's masterpiece; Beauty's centrepiece.[3]

"In Eden, the garden of God," humanity was *"perfect in beauty,"* adorned with *"every precious stone."*[4] Tragically

though, Yahweh explained to Ezekiel, *"your heart became proud on account of your beauty."*[5]
Pride in our outward beauty corrupted our inner beauty.
Which is why, to protect us, our outward beauty fades.
Our outward *"beauty is fleeting."*[6]
Delicate and fragile.
It can be smashed; smeared.
Trampled; torn.
Disfigured; demolished.
Envious onlookers hailed Jerusalem as the *"perfection of beauty."*[7]
Yet this *"splendour"* was brought crashing down.[8]
Because of its lack of inner beauty.
Because of its sin; its inner ugliness.[9]
Outwardly, King Saul was *"as handsome a young man as could be found anywhere in Israel."*[10] Inwardly though, he was selfish and afraid, paranoid and bitter, volatile and vengeful. So Saul's lineage and legacy was torn from him and transferred to David: a man shimmering with inner beauty; *"a man after God's own heart."*[11]
Because *"people look at the outward appearance, but God looks at the heart."*[12]
The staining and smearing, soiling and sullying of our inner beauty is what makes us incompatible with God, the complete and utter fullness of inner – invisible and intangible – Beauty.
When Yeshua became physical – visible and tangible – a key messianic prophecy of Isaiah, which declares that *"he was pierced for our transgressions,"*[13] also asserts that *"he had no beauty or majesty to attract us to him, nothing in his appearance that we should desire him."*[14]
Being fully God, didn't give Jesus outward beauty.

But it did mean he was filled to overflowing with inner beauty.

And in his death, Jesus was pummelled and disfigured, mangled and torn, stained and smeared, soiled and sullied – Jesus became ugly – *"to bestow on us a crown of beauty instead of ashes."*[15]

Our hideous sins were laid *"on"* Jesus.[16]

And *"in"* Jesus.[17]

To restore the fullness of our beauty, inside and out.

It's possible to speculate that the resurrected Jesus was transformed in appearance, not initially recognisable, because as the first *"fully restored"* human[18] he was suddenly beaming with outward, physical beauty.

Indeed, John's vision of the ascended, glorified Jesus – the Bible's only direct description of Jesus' physical appearance – is a masterful artwork in itself, with hair *"as white as snow,"* eyes *"like blazing fire,"* and feet *"like bronze glowing in a furnace."*[19]

Elohim is now blazing and glowing with physical, visible beauty. And in the future, so can we.[20]

"How attractive and beautiful they will be!"[21] proclaimed Zechariah.

"The Branch of Yahweh will be beautiful and glorious," cheered Isaiah.[22]

Until then though, Peter warns us, *"Your beauty should not come from outward adornment... rather, it should be that of your inner self, the unfading beauty of a gentle and quiet spirit."*[23]

Ruach is working to restore and transform our solid physicality – coaxing beauty out of the dust – by first breathing beauty into the dust, immersing and imprinting, instilling and infusing.

Like Elohim at the very beginning of time, invisible inward

beauty must be the springboard for visible outward beauty. Breathed out in the image of Beauty, we are commissioned to become beauty-makers.

Beauty-restorers.

Beauty-nurturers.

Which is why Solomon's Temple abounded with ornate carvings of trees and fruit and flowers[24] and beasts, alongside thousands – literally thousands – of baths or basins of water.[25] It was an immense complexity producing a blissful simplicity which would have felt like walking through paradise.

Bringing a glimpse of heaven.

Transfixed and transported by a majestic vision of God – *"high and exalted, seated on a throne"* in a temple[26] – Isaiah heard a sensational serenade, singing, *"Holy, holy, holy is Yahweh Almighty."*[27]

Similarly, eight centuries later, transfixed and transported by a dazzling vision of God – *"with the appearance of jasper and ruby"*[28] – John heard a sensational serenade, singing, *"Holy, holy, holy is the Lord God Almighty."*[29]

The first Christians saw the triple repetition of 'holy' as a veiled Trinitarian allusion; a hidden hint or clue.

Abba, Yeshua and Ruach are 'holy, holy, holy.'

A paradise of pure perfection.

Absolute heavenly Bliss.

Filled with beauty.

And goodness.

And peace.

And truth.

And life.

The angelic acclamation heard by Isaiah immediately preceded the refrain, *"who was, and is, and is to come"*;[29] while

John's proclaimed: *"the whole earth is full of his glory."*[30]
The message was clear: being 'holy, holy, holy' did not mean isolation, keeping away, afar, apart for fear of cross-contamination. Being 'holy, holy, holy' meant moving towards us; coming close. The eternal, ethereal God who is total Bliss intends to fully immerse and inhabit a physical world of heavenly bliss.

A cosmic paradise of utter perfection.
An absolute masterpiece.
Filled with beauty.
And goodness.
And peace.
And truth.
And life.

When heaven infuses earth, absolute Bliss will look us in the eye and euphorically announce, *"Truly I tell you, today you will be with me in paradise."*[31]

When heaven and earth become one, immaculate Beauty will pull us into Elohim's embrace and sing, *"You are altogether beautiful, my darling; there is no flaw in you."*[32]

1. Psalm 27:4
2. Psalm 50:2
3. Ephesians 2:10
4. Ezekiel 28:12-13
5. Ezekiel 28:17
6. Proverbs 31:30
7. Lamentations 2:15
8. Lamentations 3:18
9. Lamentations 3:42
10. 1 Samuel 9:2
11. 1 Samuel 13:13-14
12. 1 Samuel 16:7
13. Isaiah 53:5
14. Isaiah 53:2
15. Isaiah 61:3
16. Isaiah 53:6
17. 1 Peter 2:24
18. 2 Corinthians 13:9
19. Revelation 1:14-15
20. Revelation 21:2
21. Zechariah 9:17
22. Isaiah 4:2
23. 1 Peter 3:3-4
24. 1 Kings 6:18-35
25. 1 Kings 7:25-26
26. Isaiah 6:1
27. Isaiah 6:3
28. Revelation 4:3
29. Revelation 4:8
30. Isaiah 6:3
31. Luke 23:43
32. Song of Songs 4:7

God is Bliss: Peace

For most ancient civilisations, the world began via violence.
Whether it was the Greeks' familial conflicts of Zeus et al.
Or the Babylonians' Marduk tearing apart Tiamat.
Violence was in the image of the gods.
Violence underpinned reality.
Genesis' poetic opening told a radically different story.
With the cosmos emanating from Bliss.
Through words spoken in unison.
Agreement and harmony.
Violence originated from human choice alone.[1]
With familial conflict quickly escalating.
Into vicious bloody murder.[2]
"Anyone who kills Cain will suffer vengeance seven times over,"[3] Bliss warned in an attempt to suppress the inaugural violence. But when Lamech avenged injury with murder, the killer scoffed, *"If Cain is avenged seven times, then Lamech seventy-seven times."*[4]
Violence was spiralling.
And before long, it was everywhere.[5]
Which begs the question: how would, how could, how should *"the God of peace"*[6] respond to a created realm now so tragically, horrifically and diametrically different to his nature?
Genesis answers: grief.
Sorrow.
Horror.
Regret.

Remorse.[7]
All overflowing into the flood.[8]
Abba, Yeshua and Ruach's own inaugural act of violence was, to an extent, unsurprising. It was an extreme and devastating response to an extreme and devastating situation. What was surprising however is that Elohim didn't choose to start again with freshly-breathed humans – or even give up on humanity altogether – but rather reset with an existing family. Indeed, Noah's enormous vessel could have potentially saved hundreds, perhaps even thousands – all with worse flaws than Noah – had they decided to board.
And then, despite the sheer inevitability of humanity starting another self-destructing downward spiral,[9] God said, *"Never again."*[10]
The flood was a standalone, one-off attempt at shaking and awakening a sleep-walking, slumbering humanity, striving to open eyes to the consequences of such proliferating violence.
Because Peace desires peace.
And Peace is pursuing peace.
One of the essential takeaways from Abraham's dramatically aborted sacrifice of Isaac was: *"Do not give any of your children to be sacrificed."*[11] The abhorrent, widespread practice was, wept Yahweh, *"something I did not command or mention, nor did it enter my mind."*[12]
Which is why a detailed system for offering animals was established.
To help deflect and placate humanity's perverted urge.[13]
This was progress.
Still far, far, far from ideal.
But an important step forward.

Out of the many incidences of Bliss inciting and initiating violence, perhaps the most horrific is the Israelites' conquest of Canaan. Even so, it's important to note that in a world where manic, merciless massacres were common, Yahweh's offensive was radically different. First, those unwilling or unable to fight, for whatever reason, were invited to excuse themselves.[14] Next, attacks themselves required divine – not human – instigation, and were strictly limited to set times and locations.[15] And finally, before attacking, there should always be an offer of peace; an opportunity to surrender.[16]

This was progress.

Still far, far, far from ideal.

But an important step forward.

And surely, given Yahweh's recent history of splitting seas and humiliating Egypt, surely surrender was the obvious, inevitable choice.[17]

Wasn't it?

But to Yahweh's horror, *"except for the Hivites living in Gibeon, not one city made a treaty of peace with the Israelites."*[18] So the Israelites were told to *"drive out"* existing inhabitants;[19] or more occasionally, to *"annihilate"*[20] and *"completely destroy."*[21] At least four hundred years in the waiting,[22] the invasion sought to eradicate *"all kinds of detestable things* Yahweh *hates,"* including the abominable burning of *"sons and daughters… as sacrifices."*[23]

Centuries later, through Amos, the embracing Elohim again declared violent judgement on Israel's surrounding neighbours. Various military fortresses would be consumed by fire.

For taking and selling captives.[24]

For *"disregarding a treaty of brotherhood."*[25]

For wildly slaughtering with *"unchecked"* fury.[26]

For "ripping *open the pregnant women of Gilead.*"[27]
For burning Edom's King.[28]
But then, receiving no favouritism, attention turned to Judah and Israel. For their own crimes against humanity, their own *"fortress of Jerusalem"* would also be consumed.[29]
Turning a blind eye to Amos' warnings – or perhaps even laughing in the face of them – two of Judah's subsequent Kings even burnt their own offspring as offerings[30] to other nations' gods.[31]
So, overflowing from Yahweh's inconceivable grief, another shaking, another awakening began.
Because the purpose of divine anger, divine violence, divine punishment is always the pursuit of peace. Painful discipline, it was later realised, has the potential to produce *"a harvest of righteousness and peace."*[32]
And sure enough, from the utter pain and agony of Jerusalem's rubble, an astonishing assertion arose: *"So great is his unfailing love. For he does not willingly bring affliction or grief to anyone."*[33] Or as another translation puts it, *"He does not afflict from his heart."*[34]
Anger and affliction are alien to Elohim's eternal essence.
Instead, punishments are provoked.
Slowly; reluctantly.
Sorrowfully; regretfully.
While peace, in absolute contrast, freely and lavishly gushes out.
"I take no pleasure in the death of anyone,"[35] Yahweh told Ezekiel.
For in the heart of Elohim every death hurts.
Every death is grieved.
Stepping into a bloody and violent world, Yeshua came to *"guide our feet into the path of peace."*[36] Juxtaposing and

reversing Lamech's threat of vengeance 'seventy-seven times,' the *"Prince of Peace"*[37] urged forgiveness *"seventy-seven times."*[38] Whereas an 'eye-for-an-eye'[39] had been an important step forward in restricting violence, Jesus went further: don't hit back at all.[40]

Absorb the violence.

Take the violence out of circulation.

When Jesus demonstrated Yahweh's anger at injustice, he never physically hurt someone, but he did hurt economically and – to an extent – emotionally. Overthrowing market stalls[41] and calling out *"hypocrites,"*[42] he was the pioneer of the non-violent protest.

Then on the brink of battle, Jesus yelled, *"Put your sword away!"*[43]

Before surrendering to punch after punch.

Rip after rip.

Slice after slice.

Feeling the full force.

Of humanity's cruellest violence.

"Like the days of Noah," Yahweh told Isaiah, *"I have sworn not to be angry with you, never to rebuke you again... My unfailing love for you will not be shaken nor my covenant of peace be removed."*[44]

Absorbing all of Elohim's anger over our violence, Yeshua made a covenant with Abba and Ruach to never punish and rebuke humanity again. Swallowing and subsuming every provoked rebuke, Peace made peace with Peace.[45]

Before declaring not once.[46]

Not twice.[47]

But three times: *"Peace be with you."*[48]

Inaugurating a new era where *"we have peace with God."*[49]

A new era where Jesus promises, *"My peace I give you,"*[50] as

Ruach proceeds from Abba and Yeshua's love to reside within us, transforming hearts and minds with *"the peace of Christ."*[51]

Two millennia later, we still live in a world of war and violence; a world clamouring for the most damaging weapons; a world governed by the threat of 'You bomb us, we'll bomb you seven – perhaps seventy-seven – times harder.'

"God has called us to live in peace,"[52] Paul wrote. So *"make every effort to do what leads to peace.*[53] *Do not take revenge, my dear friends, but leave room for God's wrath, for it is written: 'It is mine to avenge; I will repay.'"*[54]

So every time we trust in Elohim to deal with justice.

Every time we surrender our impulse to retaliate.

Every time we *"pray for those who mistreat"* us.[55]

Every time we refuse to *"repay evil with evil."*[56]

Every time we love our enemies.[57]

This is progress.

Another step forward.

In Elohim's long-enduring pursuit of peace.

Because in Yahweh's vision of the future, swords are turned *"into ploughshares"* and *"spears into pruning hooks."*[58] And more than ever we need to take violence out of circulation and transform vile, destructive weapons into tools for caring for creation.

Pursuing not just an absence of violence, but 'shalom.'

Absolute fullness and wholeness.

Absolute bliss.

Bliss: Peace

1. Genesis 3:16
2. Genesis 4:10
3. Genesis 4:15
4. Genesis 4:23-24
5. Genesis 6:5
6. Romans 15:33
7. Genesis 6:6
8. Genesis 6:7
9. Genesis 8:21
10. Genesis 9:11
11. Leviticus 18:21
12. Jeremiah 19:5
13. Psalm 40:6
14. Deuteronomy 20:5-8
15. Deuteronomy 2:4-19
16. Deuteronomy 20:10-12
17. Joshua 2:9-13
18. Joshua 11:19
19. Joshua 3:10
20. Deuteronomy 9:3
21. Deuteronomy 20:17
22. Genesis 15:16
23. Deuteronomy 12:31
24. Amos 1:6
25. Amos 1:9
26. Amos 1:11
27. Amos 1:13
28. Amos 2:1
29. Amos 2:5
30. 2 Kings 16:3
31. 2 Chronicles 33:6
32. Hebrews 12:11
33. Lamentations 3:32-33
34. Lamentations 3:33 (ESV)
35. Ezekiel 18:32
36. Luke 1:79
37. Isaiah 9:6
38. Matthew 18:22
39. Exodus 21:24
40. Luke 6:29
41. Matthew 21:12
42. Matthew 15:7
43. John 18:11
44. Isaiah 54:9-10
45. Colossians 1:20
46. John 20:19
47. John 20:21
48. John 20:26
49. Romans 5:1
50. John 14:26-27
51. Colossians 3:15
52. 1 Corinthians 7:15
53. Romans 14:19
54. Romans 12:19
55. Luke 6:28
56. 1 Peter 3:11
57. Matthew 5:44
58. Micah 4:3

God is Bliss: Life

Before the beginning of time, before the creation of solid physicality, there was life.
Abundant life.
Life in all its fullness.
Throbbing and brimming with profuse frenetic, pulsing, electric, animating energy – possessing no degree of decay – Elohim's perfect blissful essence is entirely self-sufficient, requiring no outside source, relying on no grain of regeneration; no iota of recharging. Yahweh is not one superior life among, or above, a multitude of other lesser lives. 'I am who I am' is instead a whole other category of being.
Being itself.
Life itself.
The one – or the all-encompassing everything – in whom *"we live and move and have our being,"*[1] surrounding and pervading, underpinning and propelling every other living thing.[2]
Elohim is the *"author of life"*[3] who both *"gave life to everything"*[4] and *"gives life to everything."*[5] The whole of creation is wholly dependent upon remaining connected[6] to life's abundant, extravagant source.
Upon receiving life.
Gushing out.
Jetting out.
From *"the fountain of life."*[7]
Or as Job so poetically posed, *"From whose womb comes the*

ice? Who gives birth to the frost?"[8] Because our fragile, precious, momentary lives are a gift from the womb of limitless, imperishable Life. Elohim is our birth Mother who not only brings us into the world, but also desires our growth, tenderly ushering us, encouraging us, guiding us in the *"paths of life"*;[9] setting *"before us the way of life and the way of death."*[10]

"Choose life,"[11] Moses implored; and in the subsequent centuries, his cry reverberated like an accompanying drumbeat as Abraham's descendants swung back and forth between pursuing 'life' and shadowing 'death.' Yet even in their darkest days, down in the depths of death, the drumbeat – or rather Elohim's heartbeat – was still perpetually, passionately pounding: 'Choose life, choose life.'

Via Jeremiah, Yahweh explained: *"I am setting before you the way of life and the way of death. Whoever stays in this city will die by the sword, famine or plague. But whoever goes out and surrenders to the Babylonians… will live."*[12]

And sure enough, dwelling in Babylon, the deported exiles not only survived but thrived; and upon returning home decades later, Ezra celebrated that Elohim *"has granted us new life."*[13]

Before *"the way"* and *"the life."*[14]

The *"light of life"*[15] and *"the bread of life."*[16]

Fully embraced our world's cycles of decay and regeneration, where survival is dependent upon frequent refuelling, feeding on energy received by another aspect of creation, itself either killed or cut off from the source of life.

And on the night of his arrest, Jesus drew his followers' attention to a prophecy of Isaiah,[17] where a man – who'd grown up *"like a root out of dry ground"* – is *"oppressed and*

afflicted" and *"cut off from the land of the living."*[18]
There is no indication in Scripture that creating and sustaining life is, in itself, costly or painful to God; it is a natural, joyful overflow of Elohim's lavish, gushing heart.
But to bring us into a share of their own limitless, everlasting life cost Abba, Yeshua and Ruach everything; the deepest of sharpest, darkest pain.
Bliss chose to suffer.
Life – extravagant, effusive, immortal, invincible Life – chose to die.
Another prophecy of Isaiah – quoted by Matthew for finding fulfilment in Jesus[19] – goes on to dramatically and graphically announce: *"For a long time I have kept silent, I have been quiet and held myself back. But now, like a woman in childbirth, I cry out, I gasp and pant."*[20]
On the cross, Jesus cried, gasped and panted a Psalm which proclaims *"you brought me out of the womb"* and cared for me *"at my mother's breast."*[21]
Because, naked and bloodied.
Contorted and anguished.
Groaning and bellowing.
Jesus was like a woman writhing in labour.
Screaming in seething agony.
To deliver *"new life."*[22]
Seeing Yeshua, their beloved, "pouring *out his life unto death,"*[23] Abba and Ruach wailed and roared. With the fullness of God in human flesh laying limp and lifeless, the fullness of God unbounded by flesh wept and grieved, feeling the full force of Yeshua's death within them.
Isaiah declared that, *"after being assigned a grave,"*[24] the one who suffered *"will see the light of life."*[25]
And so it proved.

As Life burst forth from the ground.
Bringing *"life to the dead."*[26]
Releasing life *"to the full."*[27]
Existing from *"everlasting to everlasting,"*[28] Yeshua is the source of *"a spring of water welling up to eternal life."*[29] Having given birth to our beginning, he can give us no end, permanently imprinting our names in *"the book of life."*[30] Because fragile, limited life is a gift we have all received; while a *"new birth"*[31] into eternal, incorruptible life is a gift we are all offered;[32] a gift we can all choose.
Choose life.
Choose life.
Peter understood that those who have been *"born again"* into *"imperishable"* life[33] should, *"like newborn babies, crave pure spiritual milk."*[34] They are to become like suckling newborns in Elohim's arms; or like chicks gathered under mother-hen's wings,[35] wholly dependent, reaching out, crying out for our Mother's nourishment and sustenance.
Choose life.
Choose life.
Creation is *"groaning,"* Paul explained, *"as in the pains of childbirth"* while *"we ourselves... groan inwardly,"* and Ruach simultaneously, *"intercedes for us through wordless groans."*[36] So now, conjoined intimately with the rushing, rousing, electrifying energy of Life herself, we are commissioned to join Ruach in the ongoing throes of her labour, crying, groaning and panting to give birth to the new creation. United with Life, we cry out for all to *"receive the crown of life."*[37]
Choose life.
Choose life.
"The Spirit gives life,"[38] Jesus declared, while Paul

elaborated, *"The Spirit who gives life has set you free.*[39] *Even though your body is subject to death because of sin, the Spirit gives life because of righteousness."*[40]

Ruach brings us righteousness and resurrection.[41]

Because of Jesus' righteousness and resurrection.[42]

Choose life.

Choose life.

When the first humans chose to eat from the tree that leads to death,[43] a flashing security fence was placed around *"the tree of life."*[44] By obstructing access, the fullness of Life prevented sin-infested humans from living forever, and in doing so, avoided the irreversible nightmare of a fallen eternity.

With unending sickness.

Frailty.

And decay.

Jesus' execution on a severed, decaying tree – and his subsequent resurrection, rising from the soil – both *"destroyed death"* and *"brought life."*[45] With Jesus' sinless bliss transferred and transmitted to us, dropped and draped upon us, instilled and infused within us, the tree of life's protective barrier is obliterated; rendered obsolete. So now all can feast on its fruit without restraint.[46]

Choose life.

Choose life.

Standing plush – prominent and eminent – *"on each side"* of the invigorating *"river of the water of life,"*[47] the tree of life's fruit will be universally and lavishly available.[48] Every bite will bring us *"life that is truly life."*[49]

With no sickness.

No frailty.

No decay.

Self-sustaining limitless Life will fully fill creation.
Intimately indwelling and endlessly energising.
Every bite will bring us bliss.
Choose Life.
Choose Life.
Choose Life.

1. Acts 17:28
2. Job 12:10
3. Acts 3:15
4. Nehemiah 9:6
5. 1 Timothy 6:13
6. John 15:4-5
7. Psalm 36:9
8. Job 38:29
9. Proverbs 2:19
10. Jeremiah 21:8
11. Deuteronomy 30:19
12. Jeremiah 21:8-9
13. Ezra 9:9
14. John 14:6
15. John 8:12
16. John 6:35
17. Luke 22:37
18. Isaiah 53:2-8
19. Matthew 12:17-21
20. Isaiah 42:14
21. Psalm 22:9
22. Acts 5:20
23. Isaiah 53:12
24. Isaiah 53:9
25. Isaiah 53:11
26. Romans 4:17
27. John 10:10
28. Psalm 90:2
29. John 4:14
30. Revelation 3:5
31. 1 Peter 1:3
32. John 3:16
33. 1 Peter 1:23
34. 1 Peter 2:2
35. Matthew 23:37
36. Romans 8:22-26
37. James 1:12
38. John 6:63
39. Romans 8:2
40. Romans 8:10
41. Romans 8:11
42. Romans 6:4
43. Genesis 2:17
44. Genesis 3:22-24
45. 2 Timothy 1:10
46. Revelation 2:7
47. Revelation 22:1-2
48. Revelation 21:6
49. 1 Timothy 6:19

Logos

God is Logos: Communication

From intimate relations to international relations, communication is key. Clarity, frequency and honesty are all crucial for strengthening the invisible, relational bonds between persons.

Furthering depth.

Fuelling longevity.

Fostering harmony.

For at the heart of ultimate reality, within the perfectly permeating relations of Elohim, there is non-stop, crystal-clear communication; the invisible outworking, or outpouring, of heart and mind. Beyond and before space and time, *"Let there be..."* was uttered with pregnant anticipation;[1] and from the womb of the Logos a universe filled with the Logos was born.[2]

Initiating.

Instigating.

Inaugurating.

Spoken words called *"into being things that were not."*[3]

Distinguishing and separating.

Bringing order to chaos.

And crafted in their creator's image, humanity's first task as co-creators[4] was to coin new words, to distinguish and separate and bring order to chaos by naming and labelling the world around them.[5]

This gift of words separated – elevated – humanity from the rest of creation. There's an extent to which many other species can empathise and understand – even communicate

– but none can get remotely close to explaining ideas and articulating complexity.
For good or for ill, our words craft our world.
They build, but also destroy.
In Eden, confusion and chaos were sown with the fateful question: *"Did God really say...?"*[6] and within a generation, deceit and lies reaped vengeance and murder.[7] As humanity continued to develop[8] – and fall – a multiplicity of languages emerged.[9]
Multiplying confusion, suspicion and division.
"God is not human, that he should lie."[10] Truth immerses and undergirds Elohim's every communicative act. Inwardly, Abba, Yeshua and Ruach sing unending words of affirmation and affection over each other, sharing limitless honesty and openness; complete unity of understanding. Outwardly, seeing the juxtaposing euphorias and agonies, compassions and cruelties, Elohim speaks rebuke and correction alongside delight and endearment.[11]
From the big picture call to Abraham – blessed to be a blessing[12] – to the minutiae detail of design blueprints[13] and societal laws;[14] from the promises of crushing judgement to soaring restoration, the whole Bible recounts God speaking into humanity's mess, wooing us forward.
Instructing, ushering, pleading.
Healing, redeeming and rescuing.
The Bible records and preserves many of the Community of Elohim's key interactions with humanity, providing continuity across generations, anchoring us within a metanarrative.
The Bible is 'theopneustos,' meaning 'God breathed.'[15]
The Bible contains words breathed out by a communicative God.

Logos: Communication

It progressively reveals who God is.
But it is not God.
Ultimately, God is beyond words. Words do a good job of describing physicality and make a start on personality and character, but even for humans, words will never fully encapsulate a person's inner being.
Very often we just don't have the words.
Like, for example, 'Word': the English translation for 'Logos.' 'Word' falls far short of encapsulating the term John borrowed from six centuries of Greek philosophy. Logos covers the reason, thoughts, meaning, plans and logic – plus words and speech – inherently present throughout the cosmos. Which means, the communicated words of the Logos are incisive, profound, purposeful and true, bringing gravitas and certainty to a plethora of promises.
Even so, all words of truth and love – whether human or divine – also possess an inherent vulnerability. Carried by outgoing breaths, our every syllable leaves us. In the image of God, we surrender control, unable to determine whether our most carefully crafted thoughts are welcomed or shunned,[16] followed or forgotten,[17] understood or misconstrued. Which is why one of the greatest arts of communication is not just knowing what to say but how and when to say it.
To Joel, the Logos promised to roar.[18]
To Elijah, the Logos whispered.[19]
But to Isaiah, the Logos disclosed, *"For a long time I have been silent."*[20]
Indeed, the Bible falls silent for four hundred years.
Before the Word became wordless.
Before the eternal Logos became an embryo.

For nine months, surrounded by the whirring, whooshing sounds of Mary's womb, the developing foetus of Jesus was unable to make a sound. Then, wrapped in his doting mother's arms, all he could do was cry. As the months passed, Mary would have savoured and celebrated every laugh, every experimental sound, every attempted word from her incarnate child who would go on to speak *"the words of God."*[21]

And even call himself, *"the Truth."*[22]

When Jesus said, *"Get up! Pick up your mat and walk,"*[23] or when he cast out spirits *"with a word,"*[24] or said *"Quiet! Be still"*[25] to a storm, these were all announcements of the arrival – the breaking out – of God's future Kingdom.

On trial.

Before Pilate.

Jesus fell silent.[26]

Then in his dying breaths.

The imperishable Word exhaled, *"It is finished."*[27]

Pronouncing the end of one era.

And initiating; instigating.

Inaugurating.

The beginning of a new realm and reality where the creative Logos announces, *"I am making everything new!"*[28]

Where *"in his love* Yahweh *will no longer rebuke* us, *but will rejoice over* us *with singing."*[29]

So, when Ruach later rushed through Jesus' waiting followers, enabling them to speak in various languages,[30] this was the start of the undoing of the babble of Babel; the beginning of a completed, rejuvenated, re-made world where all of humanity understands each other.

With Ruach's inspiration, the newly-invigorated followers scanned through the Hebrew Scriptures with fresh eyes, recognising slow-burn hints and nudges of God's trinitarian nature. They realised that *"in these last days he has spoken to us by his Son,"*[31] and endeavoured to write accounts which dramatically, explosively, threw back the curtain on Elohim's embrace.

Most notably, John opened his meticulous masterpiece by succinctly stating: the Logos *"was with God"* and the Logos *"was God."*[32] He then quoted Jesus explaining, *"I did not speak on my own, but the Father who sent me commanded me to say all that I have spoken."*[33] And likewise, the *"Spirit of Truth… will not speak on his own; he will speak only what he hears."*[34]

Elohim speaks with one united voice.

Yeshua's voice is Abba and Ruach's.

Ruach's voice is Yeshua and Abba's.

And similarly, the outward-pouring, abundantly overflowing Elohim desires to be our source, our provider of words. Commanded *"to preach to the people and to testify,"*[35] every syllable we utter has the potential to restore the world around us, speaking into the void to resurrect life. And even in our toughest moments, even when we're lost for words, Jesus promised his followers, *"The Holy Spirit will teach you at that time what to say."*[36]

In his vision which closes the Bible, John saw Jesus *"dressed in a robe dipped in blood,"* wearing *"many crowns"* and riding a white horse. John wrote that this triumphant hero is called *"Faithful and True"* and *"his name is the* Logos *of God."*[37]

Then in the Bible's grand finale, John asserts the importance of protecting and preserving its words,[38] for they *"are trustworthy and true."*[39] And he depicts the divine and human speaking together with aligned hearts and minds.

First there is unison.

With *"the Spirit and the bride"* calling as one for everyone to *"Come!"*[40]
And then there is agreement.
With Jesus saying, *"Yes, I am coming soon."*
To which John responds, *"Amen. Come Lord Jesus."*[41]
The Bible's final words focus on both humanity and Jesus coming close.
Anticipating the initiation.
Instigation.
Inauguration.
Of perpetual divine-human union.
With non-stop, crystal-clear dialogue.
Not just communication but conversation.
Shaping, suffusing and sustaining the invisible, relational bonds between us.

Logos: Communication

1. Genesis 1:3
2. John 1:3
3. Romans 4:17
4. Genesis 1:28
5. Genesis 2:19
6. Genesis 3:1
7. Genesis 4:9
8. Genesis 11:2
9. Genesis 11:9
10. Numbers 23:19
11. 2 Timothy 3:16
12. Genesis 12:2
13. Exodus 25-27
14. Leviticus 23:22
15. 2 Timothy 3:16
16. Zechariah 7:13
17. Job 33:14
18. Joel 3:16
19. 1 Kings 19:12-13
20. Isaiah 42:14
21. John 3:34
22. John 14:6
23. John 5:8
24. Matthew 8:16
25. Mark 4:39
26. John 19:9
27. John 19:30
28. Revelation 21:5
29. Zephaniah 3:17
30. Acts 2:4
31. Hebrews 1:1-2
32. John 1:1
33. John 12:49
34. John 16:13
35. Acts 10:42
36. Luke 12:12
37. Revelation 19:11-13
38. Revelation 22:18-19
39. Revelation 22:6
40. Revelation 22:17
41. Revelation 22:20

God is Logos: Consciousness

Throughout the universe's expansion, the Logos – the ultimate awareness, the ultimate consciousness – has endlessly poured out from uncreated to created. Each individual's unique, independent consciousness is a lavish gift tenderly envisioned and commissioned from Consciousness themselves.

Breaths and heartbeats may sustain life.

But it is consciousness which makes us alive.

A basic baseline of consciousness begins with our ability to sense our surrounding environment. Our bodies can detect and interpret a small fraction of the vibrating energy waves around us, seeing, for example, less than 1% of the electromagnetic spectrum, with animals picking up differing – but similarly limited – ranges.

"Does he who fashioned the ear not hear?" a psalmist rhetorically sang, *"Does he who formed the eye not see?"*[1] For indeed, Ruach, Yeshua and Abba are the source from whom all senses flow; the wellspring of the vibrating waves. Hearing without needing ears, seeing without needing eyes – the list goes on – Abba, Yeshua and Ruach don't just intellectually know about senses; they experientially know them. The sensational Elohim delights and weeps in the full multiplicity of the sensory spectrums.

To Moses, a sorrowful, empathetic Elohim explained, *"I have indeed seen the misery of my people"* and *"heard them crying out."*[2] To Noah, Yahweh *"smelled the pleasing aroma"* of sacrificed birds and animals, and responded by promising to *"never again... destroy all living creatures."*[3] Similarly, the subsequent sacrificial system stressed again and again that inflamed offerings emanated an *"aroma pleasing to Yahweh,"*[4] prompting forgiveness and withheld consequence.

It wasn't the killing of animals which pleased Yahweh; it was humanity's momentary focus on their divine devoted lover, and their rising awareness of wrongdoing.[5] Paul later realised that the purpose of Yahweh's laws for living – which included offerings – was to help us *"become conscious of our sin."*[6]

Initial realisations of the reality of God are often described as an awakening of the senses.[7]

Tasting and seeing.[8]

An opening of eyes.[9]

And the source of all senses desires to enliven our senses, to increase our awareness of the divine presence already all around us.

It's common to talk about wanting to hear God.

To see God.

To feel God.[10]

But what about tasting God?

Or smelling God?

In Hebrew, 'breath' and 'smell' are 'ruach' and 'riach' respectively; the words are linguistically linked because, of course, smelling and breathing are intrinsically linked. So when we take a deep breath and inhale Ruach through our nostrils we can seek her calming, soothing fragrance, tuning our consciousness towards her pleasing aroma.

Because, stretching far beyond the scope of our senses, consciousness is an awareness of existence; an ability to acknowledge external stimuli then process, analyse and respond. We were created with minds capable of exploring and comprehending the vast created world. *"For since the creation of the world God's invisible qualities – his eternal power and divine nature – have been clearly seen, being understood from what has been made."*[11]

On the one hand the world appears to be logical and knowable, governed by cause and effect, and remarkably simple formulas. On the other hand, the more we explore, the further we dig beneath the surface – at the subatomic level of quarks and so forth – things get weird and wild very quickly.

Every answer leads to a question.

Every discovery deepens the mystery.

And the greatest mystery of humanity is our astonishing ability to study and analyse; to take a step back; to consider and imagine. Our ability to wonder and marvel is itself a wondrous marvel.

Invisible.

Intangible.

Unlocatable.

Unexaminable.

Consciousness challenges – and largely eludes – scientific investigation. A neurosurgeon can cut open a brain and study electrical pulses to build a map of activity, but they cannot get remotely close to reading thoughts. Our ability to think and to plan, to analyse and imagine, to reason and will, to choose and commit, is a uniquely personal, private experience.

Known only – possessed solely – by the self.

Paul wrote, *"Who knows a person's thoughts except their own spirit within them? In the same way no one knows the thoughts of God except the Spirit of God."*[12]

Abba, Ruach and Yeshua's thoughts are shared completely. Known mutually – possessed wholly – among the trio.

And reaching out beyond themselves towards their heart's desire, the enveloping lovers explained, *"My thoughts are not your thoughts,"*[13] before joyfully exclaiming, *"I will pour out my thoughts to you."*[14]

Amos knew God as the one *"who reveals his thoughts,"*[15] while the Psalmists described deposited divine insights as *"precious"*[16] and *"profound."*[17]

Guiding, shaping, inspiring, propelling.

Connecting us.

Uniting us.

Ushering us into Elohim's intimate, embracing arms.

Through prayer we can deepen our awareness; alter our focus; bring clarity and perspective to our thoughts; break free of our mundane, everyday, self-obsessed consciousness and instead tether and align and unify with the greater, supreme perspective of the ultimate mind who thinks and plans,[18] hopes[19] and desires,[20] chooses and wills.

The explosion of materiality from immateriality didn't just happen inevitably, as if following a formula. Instead, it was a conscious choice, an intervening action, chosen and desired by the Logos. As the worshippers in Revelation declare, *"You created all things, and by your will they were created and have their being."*[21] Elsewhere in John's dramatic sensory vision, he hails *"the Lamb who was slain from the creation of the world."*[22]

Jesus chose to surrender to his slaughter among the foliage of Gethsemane, crying through blood and sweat and tears, *"Your will be done."*[23] But his torturous execution was also unanimously chosen among the full intimacy of Yeshua, Abba and Ruach.

Before their first creative act.
Before humanity's birth.
Before humanity's fall.
Knowing the cost, foreseeing the agony and heartbreak, the fullness of the Logos resolutely committed to relentlessly drawing alongside humanity over millennia of passionate pursuit, entering into our hardships, intimately sharing our sufferings.
Indeed, the most severe excruciating pain that we each experience is a mere fragment of a far deeper pain, a deeper suffering, a deeper heartbreak felt throughout the core of Consciousness. Peter wrote, *"It is commendable if someone bears up under the pain of unjust suffering because they are conscious of God."*[24]
Giving *"himself up for us as a fragrant offering,"*[25] Jesus became the definitive pleasing aroma, rendering the entire sacrificial system obsolete. And what's more, Jesus' breathtaking fragrance is now exhaled upon us as we become *"to God the pleasing aroma of Christ among those who are being saved and those who are perishing."*[26]
Longing for *"all people to be saved,"*[27] the consciousness of the Logos *"chose us in him before the creation of the world... in accordance with his pleasure and will."*[28]
We have all been chosen by God.
Freely, consciously, deliberately, actively, eagerly chosen.
The question is simply whether we will say 'yes' in return.
Like a single, simple lunch.
Turned into a meal for thousands.[29]
Like a wedding with water.
Turned into barrels of the finest wine.[30]
The coming kingdom will be a feast[31] – a voluptuous banquet – for our senses.[32] Previously limited senses will be

intensified; magnified; made complete.[33] Our consciousness will be intensely, acutely aware of the intimately enveloping Logos.

Logos: Consciousness

1. Psalm 94:9
2. Exodus 3:7
3. Genesis 8:21
4. Leviticus 1:9
5. Leviticus 5:4-5
6. Romans 3:20
7. Matthew 13:15-16
8. Psalm 34:8
9. Luke 24:31
10. Jeremiah 1:9
11. Romans 1:20
12. 1 Corinthians 2:11
13. Isaiah 55:8
14. Proverbs 1:23
15. Amos 4:13
16. Psalm 139:17
17. Psalm 92:5
18. Jeremiah 29:11
19. Romans 15:13
20. Hosea 6:6
21. Revelation 4:11
22. Revelation 13:8
23. Matthew 26:42
24. 1 Peter 2:19
25. Ephesians 5:2
26. 2 Corinthians 2:15
27. 1 Timothy 2:4
28. Ephesians 1:4-5
29. John 6:4-14
30. John 2:9-10
31. Isaiah 65:21
32. Isaiah 65:24
33. Isaiah 66:18

God is Logos: Wisdom

Possessing perfect wisdom, united in knowledge, Abba, Yeshua and Ruach have always existed together, wholly, equally, eternally one. The single infinite mind of the Logos exploded creation into being as wisdom poured out from Wisdom, expired and exhaled from the extravagantly extrovert Elohim.

From the complex codes written into our DNA to the sheer multitude of exquisitely precise, delicate balances and cycles which sustain and maintain life on our planet, the scientific evidence is increasingly compelling: *"By wisdom Yahweh laid the earth's foundations"*;[1] Elohim *"founded the world by his wisdom."*[2]

In the book of Proverbs, a character called Wisdom *"raises her voice"*[3] and recounts, *"When he marked out the foundations of the earth... I was constantly at his side. I was filled with delight day after day, rejoicing always in his presence, rejoicing in his whole world and delighting in mankind."*[4]

Which leaves us wondering: is this a voice from Elohim's embrace?

Is this Ruach?

Or Yeshua perhaps?

Appearing to pour cold water over this possibility, Wisdom also reveals, *"Yahweh brought me forth as the first of his works, before his deeds of old; I was formed long ages ago, at the very beginning, when the world came to be. When there were no watery depths, I was given birth."*[5]

Wisdom was 'brought forth' and 'formed' and 'given birth.'

And God, by definition, has no origin; no beginning. Nevertheless, the classic, orthodox Christian understanding of the Trinity – discussed, debated, formulated and articulated in the first few centuries after Yeshua's incarnation – is that Jesus was 'generated' and the Holy Spirit was 'spirated' or 'breathed out' from the Father.

Paul for example, triumphantly, emphatically declared Jesus as *"the firstborn over all creation,"*[6] yet clearly considered Jesus as *"being in very nature God."*[7]

The early church had to grapple with this fundamental conundrum: does generation and spiration make Yeshua and Ruach lesser than Abba?

Does it make them finite, not infinite?

Does it make them gods, not God?

The answer they decided – or realised – was 'no,' since Elohim's eternal embrace exists outside of time. Which means, despite being 'brought forth,' Yeshua and Ruach's 'origin' or 'birth' have no fixed starting point.

No beginning.

There was never a 'moment' when Abba was alone.

So indeed, unperturbed by a plethora of feminine pronouns, there are long-standing traditions of equating the Wisdom character in Proverbs with either Yeshua or Ruach. Verses such as, *"Wisdom is more precious than rubies, and nothing you desire can compare with her,"*[8] or, *"All her paths are peace. She is a tree of life,"*[9] can be read as descriptions of God herself; or they can equally be read as descriptions of the wisdom breathed out into creation, present within creation.

For Yahweh is Wisdom.

And "Yahweh *gives wisdom.*"[10]

Every living creature, *"large and small,"* was created and crafted *"in wisdom."*[11] But elevated humans were also envisioned to be filled with wisdom.

Following their Egyptian liberation, Israelite tailors were *"given wisdom"*[12] to sew lavish garments, while sculptors were filled *"with wisdom"* from *"the Spirit of God"* to cut and carve in all kinds of stone, including gold, silver and bronze.[13]

Echoing the divine creative image.

Pursuing artistry and originality.

Dreaming and designing.

To bring ideas to life.

Similarly, *"the spirit of wisdom"*[14] equipped Joshua to lead the Israelites. And when King Solomon asked for wisdom to help him govern,[15] we're told he received *"a breadth of understanding as measureless as the sand on the seashore."*[16] Nations flocked from far and wide[17] to hear his unparalleled insight and discernment, notably around issues of justice and integrity, fairness[18] and equality.[19]

Yet Solomon made some catastrophic errors of judgement.

Notably around issues of justice and integrity, fairness and equality.

Solomon spent seven years building God's Temple, but thirteen years building his own.[20] Solomon formed an alliance with Egypt, Israel's former oppressor.[21] And like Egypt, Solomon whipped his slaves[22] and worshipped hundreds of gods,[23] despite being warned, *"If you… go off to serve other gods and worship them I will cut off Israel from the land I have given them."*[24]

And so it proved; Solomon's foolishness ultimately led to Israel's destruction.[25]

Clearly, receiving wisdom and acting wisely are not one and the same. It's possible to be knowledgeable and foolish. It's possible to be intelligent and make terrible, damaging choices. For, as Jesus stressed, *"Wisdom is proved right by her deeds."*[26]

"Filled with wisdom,"[27] Jesus married his words with his actions. Even statements which completely contradicted conventional logic, like *"blessed are you who hunger"*[28] and *"the last will be first,"*[29] were affirmed by his frequent socialising with society's 'last,' evoking accusations of being a *"glutton and a drunkard."*[30]

Jesus' stories delighted and enlightened infants, yet left scholars perplexed; while his teachings cut incisively to the heart, stripping away unnecessary layers and peripherals with a favourite repeated refrain, *"You have heard that it was said… but I say…"*[31]

Jesus' message was both simpler and deeper.

And uncomfortably challenging.[32]

Leaving many baffled.

Bewildered by the origin of his wisdom.[33]

"Where can wisdom be found?"[34] Job had previously asked, musing, *"It cannot be found in the land of the living"*[35] or *"bought with the finest gold."*[36] Job could never have imagined, not even in the slightest, that one day the fullness of Wisdom, residing on earth, would be traded for thirty pieces of silver.[37]

For the counter-cultural, upside-down, back-to-front logic of the Logos was carried in fullness all the way through to Jesus' shocking death. The Messiah was meant to have been mighty; one of the greatest military leaders of all time. So the concept of a crucified Christ was wholly inexplicable.

Nonsensical.

Illogical.

Impossible.

Paradoxical foolishness.

The death of the one who cannot die – and the crushing, naked humiliation of the all-powerful – quite simply, made no sense. Yet, Paul proclaimed, it was and is the very *"power of God and the wisdom of God."*[38]

The heart of God.

The ultimate image.

The ultimate revelation.

Of who God is.

Gazing in adoration at Elohim's trinitarian embrace, Paul declared that Jesus *"has become for us wisdom from God,"*[39] while simultaneously only Ruach *"knows the thoughts of God."*[40] Then the divine outward flow pulls us inward into Abba and Yeshua's outreaching arms as Ruach whispers and rushes, flickers and dances into our minds to bring us *"the mind of Christ."*[41]

Paul wrote that he prayed *"continually"* for the Ephesians and Colossians[42] to be given the *"Spirit of wisdom."*[43] Similarly, James urged, *"If any of you lacks wisdom, you should ask God, who gives generously."*[44]

Because Wisdom never forces or imposes.

Never arrives uninvited.

She patiently waits to be sought.

"Pure" and *"peace-loving, considerate, submissive, full of mercy and good fruit, impartial and sincere,"*[45] we urgently need more divine wisdom in every area of life. To restore and repair and re-create our aching, groaning world, we need more 'metanoia'; more renewal of our minds[46] – more of the eternal Logos dwelling in our brains, pulsing through the neurons, aligning and infusing our thoughts, hopes and yearnings with *"the depths of the riches of the wisdom and knowledge of God!"*[47]

Logos: Wisdom

1. Proverbs 3:19
2. Jeremiah 10:12
3. Proverbs 1:20
4. Proverbs 8:29-31
5. Proverbs 8:22-24
6. Colossians 1:15
7. Philippians 2:6
8. Proverbs 8:11
9. Proverbs 3:17-18
10. Proverbs 2:6
11. Psalm 104:24-25
12. Exodus 28:3
13. Exodus 35:31-32
14. Deuteronomy 34:9
15. 1 Kings 3:9
16. 1 Kings 4:29
17. 1 Kings 4:34
18. Proverbs 11:1
19. Proverbs 22:2
20. 1 Kings 6:38-7:1
21. 1 Kings 3:1
22. 1 Kings 12:11
23. 1 Kings 11:8
24. 1 Kings 9:6-7
25. 1 Kings 11:11
26. Matthew 11:19
27. Luke 2:40
28. Luke 6:21
29. Luke 13:30
30. Luke 7:34
31. Matthew 5:21-47
32. Matthew 5:48
33. Matthew 13:54
34. Job 28:12
35. Job 28:13
36. Job 28:15
37. Matthew 26:15
38. 1 Corinthians 1:23-24
39. 1 Corinthians 1:30
40. 1 Corinthians 2:11
41. 1 Corinthians 2:16
42. Colossians 1:9
43. Ephesians 1:17
44. James 1:5
45. James 3:17
46. Romans 12:2
47. Romans 11:33

With Us

God is With Us: Collaboration

Three individuals with distinct roles working towards an agreed ambition, with aligned hearts and minds, Elohim's very being is a seamless collaborative relationship. Eternally loving each other *"before the creation of the world,"*[1] Yeshua, Abba and Ruach resolutely, absolutely, whole-heartedly chose to become 'God-with-us.'[2]
They chose to die.
In order to choose *"us in him."*
To make us *"holy and blameless in his sight."*[3]
To give us grace[4] – and *"the hope of eternal life."*
Resolved *"before the beginning of time,"*[5] these are Elohim's transcendent plans and pledges. And they are guaranteed; predestined; unshakeable and certain.
"I make known the end from the beginning, from ancient times, what is still to come," the enveloping lovers declare. *"What I have said, that I will bring about; what I have planned, that I will do."*[6]
Some things are fixed – they definitely will happen – for they are Elohim's one-sided, unilateral, unconditional actions. But other things are possible – they may or may not happen – because they are conditional on collaboration; on freely chosen human actions.
Elohim's very first words to humanity commissioned us to become creators ourselves.[7]
We were invited to collaborate.
To work together.
To partner.

To dialogue over the unfolding future of the world.

When Abraham worried about irritating God – even infuriating God – with repetitive questions, the replies he received revealed no hint of frustration.[8] Instead, Abraham's exploration of Elohim's character simply discovered deeper and deeper mercy, to the extent that we're even left wondering whether Abraham should have enquired further.

Centuries later, Moses frequently requested – and received – mercy on behalf of the Israelites. On one occasion, the former Egyptian slaves had resolved to *"go back to Egypt,"*[9] even offensively exclaiming, *"If only we had died in Egypt!"*[10] *"How long will these people treat me with contempt,"* Elohim lamented, *"in spite of all the signs I have performed among them?"*[11] Seeing no hope for change, no hope for freely-chosen partnership, the wounded lovers of Elohim told Moses their devastated and furious conclusion: *"I will strike them down with a plague and destroy them, but I will make you into a nation greater and stronger than they."*[12]

Yahweh's overall plan remained, but this was an adjustment.

An amendment.

A reset in response to the Israelites' will.

Moses would become the new Abraham, the new father of Yahweh's light-bringing nation. Having declined this offer once before,[13] Moses again argued against the plan, pushing into Yahweh's character, begging for mercy *"in accordance with your great love."*[14]

And again, Yahweh adapted.

Adjusted.

Amended.

Rather than starting over with Moses' descendants, they

would wait for a new generation of Abraham's descendents before entering the Promised Land. From the current cohort, only Caleb and Joshua would continue into Canaan, because as Yahweh explained regarding Caleb, he *"has a different spirit and follows me wholeheartedly."*[15]

In other words, Caleb was aligned with Yahweh's vision. Caleb and Joshua[16] were collaborating, while everyone else was not.

This dynamic dialogue closely precedes a proclamation that God is *"not a human being, that he should change his mind."*[17] Likewise, the scrolls of Samuel assert, *"the God of Israel does not lie or change his mind,"*[18] while also recording an account of Yahweh adapting, adjusting; accommodating Israel's will to have a king like their neighbouring nations.

Despite being grieved by the rejection.

Despite warning of the consequences.[19]

The success and failure of Israel's Kings rested on the extent to which they chose to collaborate and align with Yahweh's global desires.

Would they use the position to benefit others?

Or abuse the power for selfish gain?

So when the first King, Saul, decided to disobey instructions, Yahweh concluded, *"I regret that I made Saul King."*[20] The Community of Elohim had been planning to establish Saul's *"kingdom over Israel for all time,"*[21] but now that privilege would pass to someone else; to someone who better reflected the divine character, with greater willingness to work towards the divine ambitions.

Again, the overall plan hadn't changed.

But the way to get there was altered.

Adjusted.

Amended.

In response to human decisions.
This is a true, genuine, alive and dynamic relationship.
Making choices in response to our free choices.
Acting in response to our free actions.
Ruach, Yeshua and Abba never change their desires and ambitions; never neglect or give up on a promise. But God does hold the next course of action lightly, ebbing and flowing, bending and flexing if required.
Indeed, the Biblical narratives contain hundreds of instances where God lays out 'if-then' options for the future. From the warning to Cain before the world's first murder,[22] to the giving of the law,[23] to the Kings of Israel,[24] through to the repeated message of the prophets,[25] the future was conditional; contingent; dependent on human choices.
"If a nation *repents of its evil*," Yahweh explained to Jeremiah, *"then I will relent and not inflict on it the disaster I had planned. And if at another time I announce that a nation or kingdom is to be built up and planted, and if it does evil in my sight and does not obey me, then I will reconsider the good I had intended to do for it."*[26]
"Perhaps they will understand," Yahweh wondered.[27]
"Perhaps they will listen."[28]
Because collaboration is far from certain.
Too often things happen that God doesn't want.
Too often, Yahweh *"looked for justice, but saw bloodshed; for righteousness, but heard cries of distress."*[29]
Because sin is all the ways that we fail to collaborate with God's vision for humanity and for the world.
While prayer is a back-and-forth dialogue reminding and realigning ourselves to the will of God.
Because God cannot – or will not – impose his will.

Instead, he chooses to inspire it.
And nurture it.
The Bible largely records the endeavours and adventures of those who said 'yes,' rather than those who said 'no.'
Jeremiah was told, *"before you were born I set you apart; I appointed you as a prophet to the nations."*[30] But were there others who had a similar calling, who just didn't respond like Jeremiah?
We partner with the embracing Elohim when our actions mirror God's actions.
Acting justly and loving mercy.[31]
Blessing as we have been blessed.[32]
Forgiving as we have been forgiven.[33]
When we work to these ends we are collaborating with the collaborative, communal God. God is seeking partners who are *"after his own heart"*;[34] who follow Jesus' example and pray[35] – sometimes in utter desperation – *"your will be done."*[36]
And through Jesus' victorious death and resurrection, Paul understood that *"no matter how many promises God has made, they are 'Yes' in Christ."*[37] Every human requirement, every covenantal obligation, every collaborative expectation, has been fulfilled by Mary's firstborn.[38]
By Immanuel: 'God with us.'[39]
By the complete divine-human collaboration.
So now, with Ruach within us helping to align our will with God's,[40] we too can become a divine-human collaboration, working towards Yahweh's ambitions.
Not because we have to.
But because *"God is for us,"*[41] cheering us on.
And because it is a good, glorious, life-bringing thing to do.
Jesus commissions us to *"make disciples"* who will *"obey."*[42]

And to be his *"witnesses... to the ends of the earth."*[43]
And like a novice learning to dance with a champion virtuoso, collaboration will be invariably messy; there will be twists and turns, trips and falls.
But the result, eventually, will be beautiful.
The hard work, pain and tears will be worth it.
This is an exponentially longer – and riskier – way to heal and restore the world than simply clicking divine fingers and imposing Paradise.
But it is the way of Love.

With Us: Collaboration

1. John 17:24
2. 1 Peter 1:20
3. Ephesians 1:4
4. 2 Timothy 1:9
5. Titus 1:2
6. Isaiah 46:10-11
7. Genesis 1:28
8. Genesis 18:30
9. Numbers 14:4
10. Numbers 14:2
11. Numbers 14:11
12. Numbers 14:12
13. Exodus 32:10
14. Numbers 14:18-19
15. Numbers 14:24
16. Numbers 32:12
17. Numbers 23:19
18. 1 Samuel 15:29
19. 1 Samuel 8:6-9
20. 1 Samuel 15:10
21. 1 Samuel 13:13
22. Genesis 4:7
23. Exodus 19:5
24. 1 Kings 6:12
25. Isaiah 1:19
26. Jeremiah 18:7-8
27. Ezekiel 12:3
28. Jeremiah 26:3
29. Isaiah 5:7
30. Jeremiah 1:5
31. Micah 6:8
32. Genesis 12:2-3
33. Colossians 3:13
34. 1 Samuel 13:14
35. Matthew 6:10
36. Matthew 26:42
37. 2 Corinthians 1:20
38. Matthew 5:17
39. Matthew 1:23
40. 2 Timothy 1:13-14
41. Romans 8:31
42. Matthew 28:18-20
43. Acts 1:8

God is With Us: Emotion

Maturing beyond the myths of their nation's gods, Greek philosophers – notably Plato and his student Aristotle – began to contemplate and conceptualise a higher power, above and beyond, separate from all. Aristotle, particularly, rationalised that to be holy meant to be wholly other; remaining in a state of perfect bliss necessitated complete disconnection from disruptive external stimuli.
Emotions, Aristotle argued, belonged solely to the mortal realm.
Over millennia, this logic became almost universally embedded; commonly, often subliminally, accepted. Yet it is diametrically opposed to the view of God presented in the Bible.
Defying the strongest inclinations of human imagination and human logic, Yahweh is passionately, overwhelmingly, unanimously with us; actually, genuinely affected by us.
In evolutionary terms, sensitivity and emotions are considerably more primal, more primitive – a far earlier development – than intellect and reason. But that doesn't mean emotions should be dismissed; stifled and suppressed. Rather, the ability to connect and care and show compassion is foundational to human identity, critical to human advancement, and key to being made in the image of God.
Our emotions are a gift.
Lavishly.
Generously.

Flowing forth from an emotional God.
Standing in stark, stark contrast to the sorrowful notion of a single, isolated god – who needs to numb all emotion simply to fend off loneliness – Elohim's intimate loving unity is endlessly overflowing with pleasure.
Elation; ecstasy.
Adoration; affection.
Absolute, abundant joy.
Enraptured by each other, this is Abba, Yeshua and Ruach's timeless transcendent nature. Unchangeable, immutable, unaffected by outside influences, Elohim's embrace will always be perfect joy and perfect bliss. It cannot be harmed, it cannot be blemished.
Nevertheless, there is also a freely chosen inside-of-time immanence to Elohim's emotions. We cannot affect, alter, provoke a response from God, against God's will. But crucially, it is always God's will to be affected by us.
Grief; regret.[1]
Anger;[2] concern.[3]
Exasperation;[4] heartbreak.[5]
Sympathy; empathy; compassion.[6]
They are all divine emotional responses.
Occasionally the Scriptures explicitly state Elohim's emotions, like when we *"grieve"* the Holy Spirit,[7] or when Yahweh sang a *"lament"* over Israel,[8] or *"regretted that he had made Saul king."*[9] But more often we're required to imagine a tone of voice behind the words. For example, when Yahweh asks Jeremiah, *"What fault did your ancestors find in me?"*[10] should it be read without expression – flat, dry and monotone – or should it be dripping with grief and exasperation?
Or try this example: *"How can I give you up, Ephraim? How*

can I hand you over, Israel?... My heart is changed within me; all my compassion is aroused."[11]

There is a sense in which these expressions of emotion are anthropomorphic. They are in themselves God coming to meet us; metaphors making accommodations for our limited minds, revealing the divine in ways that we can understand. Every metaphor of God – be it Father, Husband, Lion and so on – points to a deeper truth. They do not point to something that is not true. So when we're told that God 'grieved' or 'lamented' or was 'frustrated,' these meagre words offer an extraordinary glimpse into Elohim's unspeakable, indescribable being.

Remaining in full union with Abba and Ruach, Yeshua didn't suddenly become emotional when he became human. Instead, Jesus embodied and demonstrated all of the transcendent and immanent emotions already felt by Elohim.

Prior to his incarnation, however, God did not share the bodily functions which accompany our emotions.

Hot flushes.

Sweat.

Tears.

Muscles tensing.

Butterflies in the pit of our stomach.

Rushes of hormones and endorphins.

But Love desired to know us fully, to be with us fully, so chose in the course of time to become *"fully human in every way,"*[12] to fully know the human experience, to truly know the sweat that comes with anguish[13] and the tears that come with grief.[14]

Significantly though, to remain entirely sinless,[15] there is a further category of emotions which Jesus did not feel.

These fallen emotions are perversions.
Lust: deformed from desire.
Greed: morphed from jealousy.
Rapid-fire rage: warped from slow-burning, long-suffering anger.

The indwelling Ruach seeks to heal and transform and restore these corrupted emotions within us; alongside helping our emotions to become less volatile.

After all, Elohim's emotions do not swing from ecstatic joy one moment to devastation the next. Instead, every immanent emotion is simultaneously accompanied – or better, transcended – by joy.

Which is why Paul implores us to feel and know joy irrespective of circumstance;[16] to reflect the divine image and overflow with transcendent joy *"in the midst of a very severe trial."*[17] Paul praised the Thessalonians: *"You became imitators of us and of the Lord, for you welcomed the message in the midst of severe suffering with the joy given by the Holy Spirit."*[18]

As joy increases, fear decreases to the point – the extremity – that Joy herself, the fullness of joy and source of all joy, contains not even a microscopic or subatomic dot of fear. Fear causes division – a distancing of persons – so there is no fear between the perfectly permeating, infused and intimate relations of Love. Or more succinctly: *"There is no fear in love."*[19]

Again and again, throughout the Bible, Elohim's repeated refrain was *"do not be afraid."*

To Abram;[20] Hagar.[21]
Isaac;[22] Jacob.[23]
Moses;[24] Joshua.[25]
Elijah;[26] Hezekiah.[27]

David;[28] Solomon.[29]
Jehoshaphat;[30] Daniel.[31]
Multiple times each to Isaiah, Jeremiah, Ezekiel, Joel and Zechariah.
Mary;[32] Joseph.[33]
Paul;[34] John.[35]
And most notably of all, Jesus uttered *"do not be afraid"* to his followers, shortly before his crucifixion[36] and immediately after his resurrection.[37]
Jesus was *"full of joy through the Holy Spirit."*[38]
Likewise, Paul and Barnabas *"were filled with joy and with the Holy Spirit."*[39]
For joy is discovering God.[40]
Joy is marvelling upon her beauty.
Joy is joining hands with Joy's Embrace.
And receiving overflowing and infectious joy.
Joy is knowing that one day joy will be everywhere.
Knowing that every tear will be wiped away.[41]
Including God's tears too.
For when the world is made new, Elohim's in-time immanent emotions will no longer be necessary. There will be no more anger and frustration; not even sympathy and compassion. United together in blissful intimacy, creator and created, lover and beloved will be entirely and exclusively immersed by Elohim's timeless, transcendent emotions.
Rhapsody; delight.
Wonder; amazement.
Exhilaration; euphoria.
The world and everyone in it will be thoroughly submerged with joy.

With Us: Emotion

1. Genesis 6:6-7
2. Exodus 32:10
3. Exodus 3:7
4. Isaiah 5:4
5. Numbers 14:27
6. 2 Kings 13:23
7. Ephesians 4:30
8. Amos 5:1
9. 1 Samuel 15:35
10. Jeremiah 2:5
11. Hosea 11:8-9
12. Hebrews 2:17
13. Luke 22:44
14. John 11:35
15. 1 Peter 2:22
16. Philippians 4:4
17. 2 Corinthians 8:2
18. 1 Thessalonians 1:6
19. 1 John 4:18
20. Genesis 15:1
21. Genesis 21:17
22. Genesis 26:24
23. Genesis 46:3
24. Exodus 21:34
25. Joshua 1:9
26. 2 Kings 1:15
27. 2 Kings 19:6
28. 1 Chronicles 22:13
29. 1 Chronicles 28:20
30. 2 Chronicles 20:15
31. Daniel 10:12
32. Luke 1:30
33. Matthew 1:20
34. Acts 18:9
35. Revelation 1:17
36. John 14:27
37. Matthew 28:10
38. Luke 10:21
39. Acts 13:52
40. Acts 16:34
41. Revelation 7:17

God is With Us: Suffering

Wrapped up within Aristotle's deeply influential convictions that God didn't have emotions was the axiomatic conviction that God couldn't suffer.
Which posed the first Christians a significant problem.
Because at the core of their faith was a Jesus who suffered.
And a Jesus who was *"the image of the invisible God."*[1]
One widely adopted – mainstream and 'orthodox' – solution to this problem has been to limit divine suffering to the incarnation; suffering became possible as Jesus *"made himself nothing by taking the very nature of a servant."*[2]
In this understanding, God suffered for us, on our behalf. Jesus *"took up our pain and bore our suffering."*[3] And having experienced excruciating physical, emotional, spiritual agony this means that God can also relate to any sufferings that we are currently going through. God can put an arm around us. God can say, 'I know how you feel.' But, in this understanding, God does not quite, not fully, suffer with us.
Not in the here.
Not in the now.
But there is an alternative approach which can affirm that Abba, Yeshua and Ruach are both transcendently beyond suffering and also deeply, immanently with us in our own suffering. In this view, God's suffering is still time-limited; it has a beginning and an end. But crucially, God's suffering didn't begin with the incarnation, but rather rebellion; rejection; the origin of sin. And it didn't end with the resurrection or ascension, but rather will end when all

things are made new; when every tear is wiped away. By broadening the time-span, any Biblical references to God's suffering outside of the incarnation no longer have to be dismissed as non-literal; as not really meaning what they seem to mean. And significantly, more personally, it means that whatever we are going through right here, right now, God is actually, acutely with us in the pain, choosing to be affected by our agony.

As well as saying, 'I know how you feel.'
God can also say to us, 'I feel it too.'
Through every depression, every loneliness, every anxiety.
Through every earthquake, every tsunami, every tragedy.
Through every murder, every injustice, every inequality.
Through every loss, every heartbreak, every hostility.
God is not just with us, but suffering with us.

When Yahweh described his own character, the first word uttered was *"compassionate."*[4] In English, 'compassion' literally means to 'suffer with'; to 'co-suffer.' In the original Hebrew, it's 'rakhum'; an intensely emotional word which is occasionally translated as *"deeply moved,"* like when Joseph wept at the sight of his long-lost brothers[5] or when a mother wailed at the thought of losing her child.[6]

'Rakhum' is linguistically linked to 'rekhem,' the Hebrew word for 'womb.' For, much like 'splagchnizomai' in Greek, the word evokes overwhelming emotions felt in the womb, throughout the bowels, or the heart, the very core, the very centre of a person's being. It's the love of a mother intensely, invisibly, unbreakably bound to their child.

Who celebrates when they celebrate.
And weeps when they weep.

Through the covenant at Sinai, Yahweh professed his inextricable bond with the Israelites, with his name – his

global reputation – becoming wedded to their actions.
Their joy was his joy.
Their humiliation was his humiliation.
Or as Isaiah put it: *"In all their distress he too was distressed."*[7]
Or as Love roared via Jeremiah: *"I wail over Moab, for all Moab I cry out, I moan for the people of Kir Hareseth. I weep for you."*[8]
Because love and suffering go hand in hand.
It is a truth at the very heart, in the very fabric of the universe, because it is a truth which overflowed from the womb of Elohim. Our love leads to suffering because we are made in the image of Love. Heartbreak, jealousy, regret, anger, grief: they all become possible as a consequence of loving a human.
After losing loved ones, after having their homes demolished, after being taken as captives – after seeing Yahweh 'defeated' and 'humiliated' – Hananiah, Mishael and Azariah could have been forgiven for thinking that Yahweh had abandoned them.
Yet remarkably, courageously, they refused to bow to Babylonian gods, even at the threat of certain death. Yet remarkably, miraculously, thrown into a blazing, killer furnace,[9] not even *"a hair of their heads was singed."*[10] While remarkably, mysteriously, a fourth figure[11] was observed beside the bewildered, trembling trio.
For Yahweh wasn't just rescuing Hananiah, Mishael and Azariah.
But Yahweh was actually with them.
In the immense, seething inferno.
In the intense, searing flames.
Through Isaiah, Yahweh declared, *"I live in a high and holy place, but also with the one who is contrite and lowly in spirit."*[12]

With Us: Suffering

The contrast here is breathtaking.
The juxtaposition: immense.
The one who dwells in bliss also dwells in suffering.
With burning compassion.
Blazing rakhum.
Blistering splagchnizomai.
When Jesus foresaw Jerusalem's forthcoming suffering, he wept.[13] When he saw Mary in floods of tears, grieving her brother, his own tears tumbled with such intensity that it astounded those around him.[14]
It was not Elohim's emotion - not Love's suffering - which was made possible by becoming human. It was the tears: the visible, physical, tangible outworking, the outpouring of Abba, Yeshua and Ruach's gut-wrenching grief which had been felt through millennia at the loss of human life.
Elohim became fully human to truly, fully, experientially know the physical aspects of our suffering.
He knew hunger.[15]
He knew thirst.[16]
He knew shards of metal slicing his flesh.[17]
And he knew pain pulsing through every sinew of his body. Unlike other covenants which were between God and humanity – requiring action on both sides – Jesus' death is a covenant between, among, and within, the Trinity. Through the cross, Abba, Yeshua and Ruach each suffered immeasurably but differently. And in the new creation, where there will be no more suffering, Jesus will forever wear the wounds that made it possible.
Slain yet alive.
Slaughtered yet reigning in glory.
Yeshua will forever be the victorious lamb.[18]
Surrounded and serenaded by unending adulation.[19]

Revolutionised by an outreaching, onrushing, indwelling Ruach, James asserted that *"pure and faultless"* faith first and foremost cares for *"orphans and widows in their distress."*[20]

While Paul, through every imprisonment and near-death escape; through floggings and beatings, one stoning, three shipwrecks; through grave danger after grave danger after grave danger; through starvation and thirst and lying naked in the cold.[21]

Paul knew Love didn't just suffer with him.

But within him.

And Paul endured it all – even found contentment[22] and purpose[23] and joy[24] through it all – because he knew deep in his gut: *"We share in his sufferings in order that we may also share in his glory. Our present sufferings are not worth comparing with the glory that will be revealed in us."*[25]

So where is God in our suffering world?

"Like a woman in childbirth,"[26] Abba, Yeshua and Ruach are screaming out beside and among us, right in our midst, knowing and feeling our every pain, crying and gasping and panting to give birth to a new creation, wailing and weeping to bring an end to suffering.

Working all things for good.[27]

Working to transform and restore.[28]

Calling us forward into every act of compassion.[29]

To reach out beyond ourselves to someone around us.

Where occasionally.

We can say, 'I know how you feel.'

And even more occasionally: 'I feel it too.'

But more often than not there will be no words.

We'll simply reach out our arms.

And embrace.

With Us: Suffering

1. Colossians 1:15
2. Philippians 2:7
3. Isaiah 53:4
4. Exodus 34:6
5. Genesis 43:30
6. 1 Kings 3:26
7. Isaiah 63:9
8. Jeremiah 48:31-32
9. Daniel 3:22
10. Daniel 3:27
11. Daniel 3:25
12. Isaiah 57:15
13. Luke 19:41-44
14. John 11:35-36
15. Matthew 4:2
16. John 19:28
17. John 19:1
18. Revelation 5:6
19. Revelation 5:13
20. James 1:27
21. 2 Corinthians 11:23-27
22. Philippians 4:11
23. Philippians 1:12
24. Philippians 1:18
25. Romans 8:17-18
26. Isaiah 42:14
27. Romans 8:28
28. Romans 5:3
29. 2 Corinthians 1:3-4

Infinite

God is Infinite: Paradoxical and Physical

From the mind-body-spirit of humans.
To the height-depth-width of space.
To the past-present-future of time.
To the red-yellow-blue of colour.
To the proton-neutron-electron of atoms.
With each proton and neutron containing three quarks.
Creation is saturated with triune fingerprints, pointing towards its source, signalling its outpouring from the three-in-one and one-in-three divine essence.
For even basic counting numbers scream out the reality of infinity. With no beginning or end, we can always add or subtract more.
While there's even an infinity of decimals between 1 and 2.
And also an infinity between 0.1 and 0.2.
And between 0.00001 and 0.00002.
And so on – for infinity.
The mind boggles.
We cannot comprehend it.
Indeed, as well as complexity.
Infinity also necessitates paradox.
We should expect it.
Not fear it.
Only with an infinite understanding of God can it be true that the Trinity created, the Trinity rescues and the Trinity restores us, while also being true that the Father created, the Son rescues and the Spirit restores us.
Only the infinite can be three and one.

Only the infinite can endlessly pour out.
Only the infinite can't be divided into parts.
Only the infinite can be 'generated' or 'spirated,' yet not have a beginning. Only the infinite can be transcendently apart, yet intimately reside within us. Only the infinite can be all-knowing and outside of time and yet be genuinely surprised. Only the infinite can feel the fullness of joy, yet also the fullness of grief. Only the infinite can exist *"before the creation of the world,"*[1] yet can grow from an embryo in Mary's womb. Only the infinite can subtract from itself to take *"the very nature of a servant,"*[2] yet remain *"the exact representation of God's being."*[3]
Only the infinite is fully love and fully breath and fully light, and the fullness of relationship and beauty and peace and life and consciousness and wisdom and communication and joy; and more.
And then there are metaphors and similes: only the infinite can meet us as father and mother and sibling and friend and spouse and king and lord and shepherd and gardener; and more. Only the infinite can be our shield,[4] our rock,[5] our tower,[6] our door,[7] our vine,[8] our *"bright Morning Star."*[9]
Or come like a dove, like wind, like fire, like water.
Or flow like a force, like energy, like electricity.
And, of course, more.
When Moses sang to the Israelites, *"You deserted the Rock, who fathered you; you forgot the God who gave you birth,"*[10] he wasn't afraid to mix his metaphors. In fact, when it comes to infinity it's imperative to mix our metaphors.
And within the mix, we must also include extremities.
Like the lion and the lamb.
It's hard to know which image of God is more terrifying and destabilising.

Is it the roaring lion rampaging ravenously?
Or the feeble, vulnerable, helpless lamb?
In John's vision of heaven, he sees both; both a powerful, majestic figure with *"the appearance of jasper and ruby,"*[11] and also *"a Lamb, looking as if it had been slain."*[12]
Both are on the same throne.
And both are surrounded by a cacophonous serenade, declaring each *"worthy"*[13] to receive *"honour and glory and praise."*[14]
What if God was only a lion? Or only a lamb?
Would we desire a relationship – or eternal intimacy – with either?
But both together, as one – wow – that's stunning.
That's beautiful.
That's relatable.
That's desirable.
So what does it mean for a finite being to be made in the image of an infinite being? And what did it mean for the infinite to become finite, to become fully human?
To answer both questions, there are two lists.
One is Elohim's unshareable, non transferrable – incommunicable – attributes, like not having a beginning, and being unchanging, self-sufficient, all-powerful, all-knowing, omnipresent.
And then there are Elohim's sharable, transferrable – communicable – attributes, like not having an end, and being just, wise, merciful, gracious, creative and truthful; as well as Ruach's *"love, joy, peace, forbearance, kindness, goodness, faithfulness, gentleness and self-control."*[15]
For Elohim, every attribute, on both lists, is infinite and boundless; while for humanity, the second list – and not the first – was poured out lavishly within us.

Through the incarnation, Yeshua surrendered most of the first list; while through the fall, our shared divine attributes became drastically, devastatingly diminished within us.
Illness and suffering entered.
And death became a reality for all.
Through the fall, we lost the fullness of our humanity.
Which is why Yeshua became fully human.
Not just human, but fully human.
Early church theologians liked to say that the divine became human to make us divine. Equally, we can also say that the divine became human to restore the fullness of our humanity.
Fully divine and fully human, Jesus makes us divine and fully human.
Through the redeeming work of Yeshua, and the restorative work of Ruach, the communicable image of God is being restored within us. Through the abundant, outreaching, extrovert, sacrificial love of Abba, Yeshua and Ruach, we are invited to desire, take hold and grow in the divine attributes that were shared with us, and not the ones that weren't.
This explains the difference between our call to become more like God, and the need to resist the serpent's temptation to *"be like God."*[16]
Yahweh doesn't say to us, 'be infinite like I am infinite.'
Or 'be all-powerful like I am all-powerful.'
But rather: *"Be holy... as I am holy."*[17]
We are called to become more like Jesus, not more like Abba.
Or in Paul's words: *"To be conformed to the image of his Son."*[18]
It's crucial to realise that, after being human for approximately three decades, Yeshua didn't then ascend

back to a preferable ethereal, immaterial state.
Jesus became human, and stayed human.
Jesus is human right now.
And will continue to be.
This has astronomical implications for us.
First, because this physical planet, filled with physical humans, will be the home address of the beyond physical, and physical, God.
And second, because there is a human in Elohim right now, sitting at the right-hand of a joyous Abba, surrounded and immersed by a jubilant Ruach; a human who bears the scars of his victory over death; a human who is advocating,[19] mediating, *"interceding,"* on our behalf;[20] a human who can make actual eye-contact with us and reach out to us with his actual, physical hand, and hold us in his actual, physical arms.
Which brings us full circle.
As we look around and wonder: really?
How?
Where?
So, to close this exploration, before we begin another.
There is light. And then there is holy light.
There is breath. And then there is holy breath.
There is beauty. And then there is holy beauty.
There are words. And then there are holy words.
There are thoughts. And then there are holy thoughts.
There is animating energy. And then there is holy animating energy.
And, of course, the list goes on.
The great mystery is distinguishing between the two. Life's great challenge is to become awake and aware of the divine presence that already surrounds us; that incessantly invites

us into Yeshua's arms.

Peter described it as participating *"in the divine nature."*[21]

And it's why Jesus prayed, *"May they also be in us."*[22]

We are invited into Elohim's 'perichoresis.'

Ushered into their choreography.

Whenever we love, whenever we put others first, whenever we are honest and open, kind and generous, humble and vulnerable, creative and innovative.

Whenever we bring light into the darkness.

Whenever we are exploring the mystery.

We are not just reflecting God.

We are joining God.

We are taking Love by the hand and joining Abba, Yeshua and Ruach in their endless, energetic, ecstatic, euphoric, exuberant, electrifying dance.

Pulling us in and sending us out.

Drawing us in and propelling us out.

And throughout it all, through every twist and turn.

We are held within Elohim's embrace.

1. John 17:24
2. Philippians 2:7
3. Hebrews 1:3
4. Genesis 15:1
5. Genesis 49:24
6. Proverbs 18:10
7. John 10:9
8. John 15:1
9. Revelation 22:16
10. Deuteronomy 32:18
11. Revelation 4:3
12. Revelation 5:6
13. Revelation 4:11
14. Revelation 5:11
15. Galatians 5:22-23
16. Genesis 3:5
17. Leviticus 19:2
18. Romans 8:29
19. 1 John 2:1
20. Romans 8:34
21. 2 Peter 1:4
22. John 17:21

Also by Pete Atkinson

The Rescue Mission:
The Bible As We've Never Experienced It Before

Printed in Great Britain
by Amazon